IMPRINTING

A Healing of the Chakras

FOUR WINDS
Publications

For information address:
FOUR WINDS PUBLICATIONS
535 W. Cordova Road
Suite 112
Santa Fe, New Mexico
postal zipcode 87501, U.S.A.

This book is printed on recycled paper with soybean ink.

IMPRINTING

A Healing of the Chakras

Received by Ceanne DeRohan

FOUR WINDS PUBLICATIONS

Dedicated to

The Healing of the Gap
and the Survival of Love

TABLE OF CONTENTS

INTRODUCTION

In the beginning, I had reverie without feeling I had to do anything, be responsible for anything or have My existence questioned in any way. I did not know there was anything other than that. I had gone through My own process of coming into existence and My own awareness of it.

I did not mind that I had existence, as long as I did not have to do anything about it other than just exist and drift in My thoughts and images. When something began to react to My thoughts and images as though they were not all the same and was forming attachments to some of them, I was not sure I liked this.

Without letting Myself dwell on it, I had formed the impression that this was relationship, and that relationship meant opinions, criticism and limitations or requirements in the form of desire for some parts of My thoughts and images and not for others. I did not see that this had anything to offer Me other than interference with My free-form drift.

From that simple mistake on My part, I had formed a bond with Body I did not realize I had formed, which was not to look at things We did not like. From there, everything felt it had to please Us, or it would not get any of My light or the form it wanted to have. It had to feel love to feel it had beauty, and We were not loving in the beginning.

That is clear to Me now, although then, it was not. Then, there seemed to be nothing wrong in doing as We were doing. We didn't have any concept of creating evil that was building a case against Us or of anything objecting to what We were doing. We did not think there was anything else there except Us, moving along in Our flow.

If We had stopped to think about it, We would probably have realized We had a place that We were in called space and a darkness Our light was shining into, but then, We did not realize it, illogical as that seems now. We had no concept of relativity, only of existence, which had just happened to Us, and We had not noticed these things yet.

The concept of a Mother who was darkness that had pulled light into existence seemed preposterous to Us. We had come, Ourselves, into existence, and that's all there was to it, or so We thought then.

We came to certain illogical conclusions in the beginning and never questioned Ourselves about them. In fact, I had the feeling I was the only One, and Body did also. I thought He was part of Me, and He thought I was part of Him, and yet We could not get an alignment because We each wanted to rule. I thought He was a boor who wanted to move past Me on anything He didn't like, and He thought I was a prude who held back for no good reason. Thus, We invented the original Spirit/Body split that has been in place for a very long time; from the beginning, in fact.

If We had had any concept of Ourselves as One, We might have had a different experience there, but We let only One voice talk at a time and never felt We had any way to come to peace with the differing viewpoints there. Thus, another struggle was put into place; the struggle for supremacy and domination. It became a terrible power struggle that gapped Us horribly from One another.

This gap is most of what this book is about; how it was put into place, what is in it and how to heal it. It affected everyone in Creation, imprinting them in ways that they have never been able to move past, no matter how hard they have tried. Consciousness was never able to overcome imprinting no matter how hard it tried, either.

Consciousness had very little room left, once imprinting was put into place. Imprinting is most of what is in the human brain and the brains of all animals, too. Imprinting is even in the plants, because it was in all of the essence and that is all there was then; essence. In differentiating itself, it did not move lovingly at first, and this is how most of the problem was put into place. The rest of it was not knowing how to move to change that, once loving presence was there.

Unfortunately, We utilized Our old and original mistake of not looking at what We didn't like. We decided not to look back. We thought that if We did not look at it anymore, it would not be there anymore. Quite simple, and an imprinting We had formed when it was happening that way.

Before there was Will presence to hold anything present, this was a major problem of Ours, yet when the Will came, We did not recognize it as anything helpful. We noticed only how the Will seemed to hold present that which We did not want to have held present and did not notice the rest, because We thought We were doing that Ourselves, already.

This lack of recognition for the Will gave Her a misinterpretation of Our presence. She thought that We were unloving toward Her and loving toward Ourselves, and recognized Her as causing only the things We did not like and Ourselves as causing only the things We did like. Thus, She saw Us as defining Ourselves as positive and Her as negative; Ourselves as good, Her as bad, in other words.

She did not like this, and neither did We, as it turned out, but We did not notice this for a long time. We thought We liked this because it gave Us someone to blame for Our own denials, and blame Her We did, for everything that went even barely, imperceptibly wrong.

We made a gap there by not recognizing Her real role. We pushed Her away from the very beginning and did not give Her Her right place. She needs to recover from this and cannot take Her right place until She does. Until the Will has recovered, the role of the Will cannot be fully understood.

It is only just now beginning to move into healing, yet the gap is more prominent than ever on Earth, and the lovelessness of people on Earth is more apparent than ever. Why is this?

The gap is only barely moving in most people, and only mildly gapped essence is coming in as of yet. That is why.

Many people who pick up these books and think they are going to read them and follow this path, do not when they feel their own gap. They stop the process as soon as they feel anything they do not like, which is anything that might make them have to take responsibility for anything in Original Cause. Their own original cause is not going to reveal itself if they do not accept My light first, and most do not even accept these stories as real yet.

This does not mean you need to pat yourselves on the back for being first and all of the other undercurrent competition issues this might evoke. It means you need to realize what a huge issue fragmentation has become on Earth and that most people don't even feel they have enough presence to move toward healing themselves yet.

This has to heal a little at a time because the gap is more frightening than many people think when they think they can heal in a short time. That is another group of quitters; those who think it is taking too much time and too much feeling bad compared to how much feeling good.

This is imprinting that will become quite obvious to you as you read this book; imprinting that checked out long ago and never checked back to see if there was anything else it needed to know. It thinks numb is feeling good and does not mind not feeling anything. This is not ready to move yet out there until it moves inside with the pieces whose rage fragments these are, and they are legion in number; most people on Earth.

The rest are moving along without knowing it and do not need to read the books because their feelings don't have that much depth to them and they do not have much responsibility, either. That leaves a rather small group who are frightened that they might have quite a lot of responsibility and have not wanted to take it in the past.

Fear needs to move here. You do have major responsibility, and you are major pieces of My lost essence that went into the gap. Your whole existence has been lived in the gap without My light there to help you much at all.

This has been a major problem for all of you, and it has become a major problem for Me, too, because I cannot move any more without your help, and you cannot move any more without Mine. It has to balance now. That is all there is left to do, or We cannot live anymore. We tried everything else first because the gap was the last place We wanted to go. Now it is the place We have to go and the only place We can go.

The fear of being crazy has to move out, too, because it is not possible to move past old imprinting without moving the gapped rage and held terror that has kept it in place for so long.

Feelings need movement. Moving them out does not mean getting rid of them anymore. It means moving out old fear patterns and letting another emotional response come in its place. It means moving in rage which was left out, feeling it had no place in Creation, not even fear's place, which was Hell.

It has a terrible feeling of no place to receive it and of pounding on the Will's held terror to make It receive it. The Will will receive this rage, but it needs another approach. It cannot give any more pain and terror to the Will and expect It to open and receive it. That is a way of giving out blame here and not looking at its own responsibility in not approaching the Will in a gentle way to begin with.

It thinks it hates gentleness more than anything else in the world as a way to avoid looking at its own responsibility here, but it needs gentleness more than anything else to heal its own feelings of displacement. It cannot both give out what it refuses to accept from others, which is blame, and expect its blame to be received before it is going to let go of blame.

It hasn't considered this, because it has been so sure it is right that it thinks it only needs to get the object of blame to realize its fault, and what? Get another agenda? Not likely, if it really is to blame, knows it and means to be.

It is not to blame. It was a major misunderstanding, but this cannot be realized unless the gap is gone all the way down through, because it does not matter what levels of consciousness realize it if it does not penetrate the gap. This We found out long ago. If consciousness could do it alone, it would have been healed long ago.

Few have wanted to go into the gap, and even fewer have returned once they have gone into it. It is a majorly dangerous place and one I do not recommend advancing on openly. Privately, in secret if necessary, healing must take place this time. If you do not think this is true, you have not been in your gap enough to know whether it is or not and have no business telling My light you know better than I do. This is an old and original position, and imprinting is the cause of it, as it is the cause of everything else that is wrong because the gap has only imprinting to go on. My light was not loving yet there. Feelings weren't accepted as having anything to offer, and so there was no Heart presence.

Does that sound like a place you want to go? I did not think so. Yet feelings are not all good, and the feelings judged against as bad are all in the gap, operating there in a state of denial without love or the light of My consciousness there with them.

That is a gap in itself; to have no love present and no light of My consciousness there, only old imprinting from before there was love. There is a major feeling in this gap that it is right and is going to prove it any time now. This is because, in this original imprinting, We had a major feeling that We were right and would have proved it if We had not been interfered with by Our other parts, which We, at that time, did not recognize as Our other parts and had surprised Us by coming out of nowhere and opposing Us.

This part of the gap has a major military build-up in place to prevent this from happening again, it thinks. It hated being interfered with when it was putting everything in place and has continued to ignore the signs and notices along the way that it needs to consider input from others.

It has gotten very clever in its fragmentation, though, and appears to be receiving input, but it is only talking to itself and does not notice there is anyone else there who has anything of value to offer or that needs to be considered. This is a very dangerous position to be in and one that almost cost My light My life and My existence in any form.

I still have a major problem to turn around on Earth, but it is going to heal. It just needs more time; the very thing you all think you do not have any more of on Earth, yet the earth changes never seem to quite happen.

They are happening. They are happening inside first and will happen very quickly in outer reality when it is the right time. I am not going to make any predictions here about when that is, because you all need to move your held stuff, or it is not going to happen for you the way you want it to, and that is all you need to know.

The rest can be left up to Me. Although that is not a favorite position of yours, it is not possible to have it another way at this time. It is necessary to move rage and terror if you do not trust Me until you can trust Me, because it is not possible to trust Me if you cannot feel that I am loving now.

I have nothing more to say in this introduction, except that I hope you move what you need to move, take responsibility for what you need to and heal the gap you need to heal at your own right speed so that My light can come into the places where it has never been before. I am ready, are you?

THE FATHER OF MANIFESTATION SPEAKS

In the very beginning of My earliest memories, there exists a feeling that I was not loving at first toward others, and that everything I did in reaction to that judgment against Myself, that said I was not loving already as I was initially, has been guilt, until I do not know how I feel anymore.

I am torn between wanting relationship and not wanting relationship if it means that I cannot have what I want to have and be the way I want to be. Only recently have I considered this reaction to be a not even knowing what I want or how I want to be other than that I want peace.

The Will never seemed to be peace to Me, and hence, I have denied it for so long I am not sure how to find it or if I even want to find it. If it is lost from Me, maybe that is best. At least, I do not feel bad, which is how I felt most of the time with the Will around. It gave Me no peace. No matter what I did, it wanted Me to be doing something else, or doing it some other way or at some other time.

The feeling was never pleasant either. It was always one of feeling that no matter what I did, it was wrong or at the wrong time or in the wrong way or wrong somehow. I could never feel right anymore, and that's why I say everything I have done since then has felt like guilt.

I never wanted to have guilt, but I never wanted to be unloving either. Being loving toward Myself meant doing what I wanted to do and that's all, but I was never able to take the step into relationship without having it feel like I was going to have to change My ways to suit the others involved, or have them change their ways to suit Me. I did not like doing this unless it felt right to Me, which it never did.

No matter where I went, someone had an opinion about what happened there or what I did that was not the same as My opinion. I could not help feeling that I did not like what they did or that their opinions did not agree with Mine. I had only My own feelings to go on, and I did not like being crossed. I hated the compromises I was forced into by feelings of not being right.

I fastened onto a fantasy relationship there in the Will, a fantasy woman who never had feelings that crossed Me or opinions other than My own. If she had anything to say, it was always complimentary and made Me feel better than I felt already.

I did not like being brought down by the Will and did not notice the Will as having anything to offer by doing this. I thought only that it had a problem going up and did not like feeling good for some reason that was inexplicable to Me, unless the reason was holding onto fear and not letting it go that held it back this way.

I tried to give the Will some reassurance, patience and even presence in that place, but I could not stay there for long because it felt so bad that I could not imagine staying there any longer than I had to. I could not imagine why the Will stayed there at all.

In the end, I concluded that the Will liked being in a state of fear, that fear must not feel the same to the Will as it did to Me, or if it did not feel altogether good to the Will, it was, at least, familiar to the Will, and that the Will preferred familiarity to feeling good which was different and unfamiliar to the Will.

I felt that the Will was free to join Me anytime it got past enough of its fear to be ready to move the way I wanted to move, but the Will did not want to take the risk of moving to another place. I secretly thought this meant that the Will would be left behind, but this has not proven to be the case, as the Will has managed to stay present in My reality for a very long time, maddeningly present, in the form of women who do not like Me or My ways. I have given them the brush-off many times, but they never leave. They do not know what is good for them, or they would not brush past Me and trigger My rage.

My rage has many faces. They are not all good, pleasant or loving, but they all reflect My need to survive, and survival, to Me, has not meant compromising the way they have wanted Me to. I do not give in easily because I never learned that as a way to survive.

Survival has always meant holding fast to what I wanted to

have and not letting go. I cannot imagine how to survive and not have power issues and issues of control with those around Me, unless, of course, I am by Myself. Any compromise that I have made has not been willing because it has not come from a feeling that I am right already. If it had, I would not be compromising. If I am right already, why do I need to compromise?

Right is important to Me because it is not possible to be wrong and have it feel good. It does not feel good to be wrong because then it means that I do not know what I am doing or how to proceed.

It is not fair to have the Will always telling Me how to do things, disagreeing with Me as to how it is going to be done and not doing these things itself. I have the body to do these things, and the Will orders Me around as though it does not have the means to do these things itself.

I do not mind helping the Will, but I do not like the way the Will treats Me, as though it should get inside of Me and be the feelings that determine My behavior. It does not seem right that a woman should run Me, and I am not going to let it happen. I don't want anyone telling Me what to do, least of all a woman. It is not possible to have a woman telling Me what to do and be a man at the same time. I have a sovereign right to Myself.

I have more rage over this than any other issue in My life; other people telling Me what to do. It does not matter anymore whether they are women or men. Rage says I need to move according to My own ideas, and they are not letting Me do this, to the point that I am no longer sure how I really feel and have to get off by Myself to determine this once again.

For Me, life has been a struggle of trying to keep My head above the waters of others trying to shove, drag, push and pull Me their way. Guilt is more present with Me now than My original light, which I feared was unloving, but now I am not so sure.

Maybe being by Myself and doing My own thing is better than all of the wrangling around people have done about how things should be done and getting nowhere, in My opinion.

I had a vision originally about how easy a flow this could have been, and this is never allowed to happen anymore. Everything is a struggle against everyone else's differing opinions, and the compromises have never felt good; only a little bit of something that never satisfies. For example, "I'll give you sex if you work all of your life to provide me with a home."

I'll have a few nights of good sex before I'm too tired from working to have sex at all, or the promise will be forgotten in the name of home maintenance or childcare.

Life sucks, and the more I look at it, the less interested I am in having it anymore. Unless I can feel good, I don't want life, and the argument that going into the bad will make it better hasn't worked. The more I look at what I don't like, the more of it there is. I have more and more bad feelings in My life and less and less of the good.

I think there is something in the Will that doesn't want to let Me feel good and hated Me for having started out that way. I have no place in Me that feels good anymore without a problem, at least next door, and I have no power to do anything about it because everyone else thinks they know more than I do, and they don't listen to Me anymore. I think they have life without Body in mind because they never appreciated Me from the beginning anyway, so why should I care what happens to them?

I felt that I had all I needed inside of Me originally anyway, and when these bothersome voices decided that they wanted Me to include them, they should have mentioned that they didn't agree with Me and just wanted to run things by taking over My show.

They had nothing going on, no light of their own, and they still don't. They are still stealing Mine as though time has not moved and evolution is not taking place. All they've done is run through all of the forms I had in Me originally and trash every one of them.

They have not made Me any nice place to live. They have used Me as a workhorse instead, as though it is their God-given right to abuse Me in the name of service to God, relationship, community, achieving their goals and whatever else they decide to say about it.

It's all the same to Me. No service is a good service if it does not take into account My needs, and My needs are to feel good and to have an easy, simple flow to life that I can maintain in peace.

Beauty is something the Will is always going on about. Nothing is ever beautiful enough for the Will, as evidenced by how many women never think they look good enough, but peace is beautiful to Me, and if it's never peaceful, it's never beautiful. How can any woman ever look good if she is always torn up emotionally about what she doesn't have or how she doesn't look?

Beauty is something that grows from peace and not the other way around. That's My feeling, and now a feeling of guilt, as though that's what the Will is somehow, is sounding like I have to qualify that as though I might not be right somehow.

This guilt has to go. Its right place is not with Me anymore. I have to move along in peace, and that's all there is to it. I never thought relationship could mean such a lack of peace, or I would not have let My fantasy woman come to life and have any Will of her own. She never let Me know what she held inside until it was too late. "You never know the Will until you get involved, and then it's too late because the Will never lets you go," is My song of the blues.

I wanted to move along on My own until I saw if what I had in mind worked or not. I was never allowed to find that out, and now, with all that has happened since, it seems too late to go back there and try to find out.

Everything that has emerged cannot just be pushed back out of existence until it feels like right time for it, if and when it ever is, but I often wish it could happen that way. I have often felt that I regretted having anyone else around. I have often felt that the others I do not like pushed their way into manifestation too quickly or pulled on Me to include them before I wanted to or was ready to include them.

I had to go through My own experience of coming into existence, and they just wanted to give Me all their problems to solve for them instead. I accuse the whole Will polarity of this in My rage.

I do not know how to balance this with their terror and their not liking where they were in the very beginning, but I no longer feel that a path of guilt that helps them all of the time at the expense of My own life is the right way, or it would have helped by now. Maybe they have some survival terror of their own to go through on the way to creating something for themselves that feels good to them.

I sound very separatist right now, and I guess that's where My needs are right now. I feel that if I do not go back to the very beginning and have it My own way there, I can never move past that place of not knowing if My way would have worked better than what happened instead.

BODY SPEAKS OF HIS EARLIEST RECALL

I was drifting in relationship with the light I had found visible when I became aware of seeing it. I was going into it and experiencing it in Me without realizing a difference between Myself and it. I was seeing a vastness of light which I felt I was in and not separate from, yet I experienced it also, as though there was some differentiation there between the light and My seeing of it.

In some way, I felt I was both the light and the seeing of it, but I did not have a particular sense of seeing Myself as differentiated from anything else there. It was as though I was the observer of the light, yet I was in the light and the light was in Me.

There was something about being there, seeing the light and yet being the light, about how big or small I really was and about My own separateness, or lack of it, that I did not comprehend. I was frightened by it. I could not understand how everything could be Me, but I thought that it was. I felt like the originator of everything, and I did not think there was anyone else there. I did not see how I could be so, as I would put it now, schizophrenic.

I pondered this for what seemed like a very long time, and then I moved away from My feelings there. I did not want to try to figure it out anymore. I just wanted to experience Myself in a drifting sea of light and see what was going to happen and what questions might get answered that way.

I was experiencing form, or physicality, already as light and the ability to see light and as an openness to forms that were already presenting within it. They were drifting, fleeting forms, but I liked watching them.

Colors began to appear in the light too, and I was fascinated by them. It was as though My fascination or focus made them more visible or brilliant, or as though they felt My love for them, and their response was to give Me more of them and to dance to please Me.

I even had the idea that if I looked away, these colors and even this light might not exist anymore. I was absorbed in a focus that I thought was even calling this into existence, or at least into coalescence and expression. I was encouraging it, you might say. I was enjoying this so much that I didn't want to look away or do anything else but drift in this sea of essence.

I ignored anything I judged might distract Me from this. What I had going on was already exciting enough without imagining anything more. My focus was to keep it going. Moving along in it seemed like the only path to take and the path that would take Me wherever I needed and wanted to go at the time that was right for Me and in the way that was right for Me.

When other thoughts began to have presence with Me, I viewed them as having come along later. They did not, at first, have anything negative to say, but nonetheless, I had a need to keep them as aspecting thoughts.

Even though they seemed to be as excited by what was happening as I was, seemed to be aspects to My own thoughts and even seemed to love what I had happening and to be coming forth in response to it, I regarded Myself as the captain of the ship and the

One who could and must be free to command it anyway I wanted to. I was the One who was there first, and I was the One who knew how to keep My reality present with Me.

Even though these additional thoughts did not disagree with Me at first, they were not quite the same as My main stream of thought and did not let Me remain as calm as I had been. They were complicating something I wanted to keep simple. It did not occur to Me that I had not let Myself notice any excitement before then, or that this might be an excitement part of Me.

This was Heart, as it turned out, but I did not know it. I did not want to allow it freedom of expression, or to let it dominate in any way. I thought I was the only One who knew how to do what I had been doing.

I was only aware of trying to focus on this reality of Mine. It was familiar and comfortable to Me and had had nothing in it that opposed Me or had a different idea of how it should look or be.

As long as these aspecting thoughts, or voices, agreed with Me, I was willing to let them be there. If they had a differing opinion or did not accept My focus wholeheartedly, I felt impatient and limited or held back in some way that I did not like. I perceived Myself to be taken out of My natural flow by differing opinions that did not know how to do what I was doing and did not understand or respect Me enough to let Me do it. I wanted to be the dominant thought pattern. I had a feeling of being interrogated, opposed, overwhelmed, intimidated and even threatened by their presence. I was building a rage there but noticed only My restless impatience.

I was sure I had to maintain My focus the way I had been to maintain what I had happening within it. I had evidence for this from times when I had experienced lapses in My focus during which I did not know what was there, if anything.

I experienced only darkness in those lapses and did not like the feeling there. I had no consciousness there that I was aware of. If anything was going on there, I did not like it as much as what I had happening in the light where I was holding My focus. There, I had dreams, and some of them did include relationship as something that moved along with Me and never differed with Me about anything.

As long as these voices, or companions of Mine, understood that I had to have My focus, listened to Me and knew when to be quiet, We had a great relationship with many good times in excited states of awareness in the light. My experience there felt good, and that was all that mattered to Me. I didn't want anything else for a long time.

ENCOUNTERING THE WILL ESSENCE

When I did awaken to having more feelings of physicality than I had been aware of before, it was to feelings of sexuality. I felt drawn by what would now be called My loins to find something that would receive Me there. I had body sensations that felt like I was becoming aware of the lower part of My Body. I had come into contact with an essence that was exciting Me. It felt like the lower part of Myself stirring Me, and I had not known it because I had been so busy dreaming in the upper half. To Me, it was as though I was suddenly adolescent and wanted to move with it. I did not want to let go of these sensations; I wanted to go into them.

I also noticed another feeling sensation there of something cozying up to Me as though it wanted to go into these feelings with Me; something that felt like a She that wanted to have sex with Me. I did not have those words then because I did not know where it was going to go, but I wanted to say it that way so that We men could notice how imprinted We have been in Our interpretations of women' s behavior, and realize how often We have not felt into it any deeper than Our original imprinted assumptions.

I wanted to move sexually. I wanted to move spontaneously. I had feelings of not being able to hold back. I was ready; even urgent. I needed to have sex.

Why wasn't She receiving Me the way I wanted Her to? Where was Her passion? I was only hearing low sighs and moans and a rocking feeling. It wasn't going anyplace I wanted it to go. Didn't She feel Me there? Didn't She understand how it felt to be Me? I moved toward Her, and a great murmuring and sighing arose, as well as sounds of pain, displeasure and even opposition. She hesitated in Her response to Me. I took it as a "no."

I did not move past Her there, but I did not like it that She did not move toward Me the way I wanted Her to. I had to move sexually and not wait anymore. I did not want to be held back. When She did not receive Me with the speed I wanted Her to, I did not move toward Her anymore. I pulled back instead.

When She moved toward Me, I did not respond anymore. Even Her touch made Me feel held back, controlled and slowed down. I had lost interest in Her already. She was just one possible pleasant sensation among many I had had already. When She sensed this, it felt as if She grew hooked claws and used them to grab onto Me and not let Me go. It even felt like She wanted to punish Me for wanting to go.

She tried to give Me millions of nuances as to why I shouldn't leave Her that way. It all felt like a sticky web of guilt to Me. I was not interested in any of it. I wanted to go right into My feelings and sensations of sexuality without thinking about it; about where it might go, what might happen, what it might mean, or if there was anything She wanted Me to do to get to know Her or to create a secure relationship within which to do this.

What was there to know? I knew Her enough to know that I wanted to move with Her sexually, or thought I did until She started with this. What else was there to know except whether I liked it or not? If She did not like it, I was going to move on until I found someone who did.

I did not have the thought that there might be repercussions from this. I was wild with excitement. I was already holding back as much as possible. I gave Her input that let Her know I did not like the hesitation She was giving Me. Either She wanted to go into this, or She did not. It was that simple. She was causing Me to lose My focus and My sensations, and I did not like it. I wanted to know Her sexually first, and She wanted commitment first.

I became confused. She was making this so complicated, when I wanted it to be simple. Why had She given Me the feeling that She wanted Me in this way and then changed Her mind?

I felt excited, driven up and rejected. I did not take Her sexually there, but My rage wanted to.

I was hurt, and then glad I hadn't gotten any more involved than I had. I thought I needed to, and could, pull out of this like pulling out of a bad dream. She was not giving Me what I wanted. She was not letting Me go. She grabbed onto Me as if She was trying to invade Me or glue Herself onto Me and come with Me instead.

I had a feeling of panic and terror that She was trying to trap Me, hold Me back, hold Me there, hold Me down, control, overrun and overwhelm Me. It felt like She needed something from Me in order to live and was trying to take it, whether I had it to give or not.

Terror came up in Me that there would be nothing left of Me. I thought I had been lured, tricked and trapped by something that wanted to drag Me down, play with Me in a cruel way, torture Me and take My life. This was not any kind of relationship that I wanted to have. I felt that My survival was in jeopardy, and that I was in danger of losing everything I had going. Feelings of suffocation and drowning came up in Me. I pushed Her away.

Fighting for My life, I rushed up and away from Her. I had a feeling there was essence with Me that didn't want to be left behind there either, but I didn't take note. I was only glad to be alive at all at the time and was rushing to get away as fast and as far from this thing as I possibly could. I was convinced that I had a black widow spider to deal with, or worse. It was monstrous and of huge proportions.

I could not have been more wrong, which I did not know until I looked back, and I did not look back until very recently. I made assumptions there, but they were fact in My mind, and they became reality; a reality I did not question until I had to. What happened there needs to be gone back over many times to find all that was put into place in that momentary encounter of drifting essence.

ANCIENT IMPRINTS SEND FRAGMENTS OUT

Drifting in, what had been so recently, a void, involved only in My reverie and with a few voices behind My ear who were agreeing with Me, observing the same things I was and enjoying them in the same way I was, I was suddenly startled and shocked into splits I did not know I was making; splits so ancient that those personifying them do not know there was anyone else there either. They think they are the oldest things in Creation also, but they do not remember it the same way I do.

They have other parts they have played, other roles they have taken and other points of view that became imprinted in them. One thing they will find, though, is that they all have the same original imprinting that I have. It all stems from this moment, no matter what tangent they have taken from there.

In the ancient, misty sea of essence, all was imprinted by this moment. I went past so many things there, I have gone back over this and over this.

I have found a sexual rage that left Me so early there I did not even know it was with Me. It was quick and heartless. It did not look to see how it was affecting anything around it. It did not care. It wanted what it wanted, when it wanted it. It has gone after women as though they have no right to stop or slow its sexual advances, and even as though they have no rights at all.

These rage fragments have made worship of body and sex their only religion. They have nothing in their mind but ancient imprinting. The imprinting there has pursued the original turn-on by attempting to recreate the original circumstances. It does not want to allow any interference to that end and goes to great lengths to ensure that.

It hates to move rage. It does not think that it needs to. It does not believe that it has any rage unless it is provoked. As long as it gets its own way, it never moves any emotion. It has a contained excitement it feels at getting its own way and a cold hatred toward those impeding it when it does not. It has conducted rapes of all sorts and concocted elaborate rituals involving the use of women.

These fragments make sure they get their own way sexually, no matter what the energy field or the signs and sounds of resistance might be. They have even drawn excitement from the rejection, the "no," and the signs and sounds of hesitation, fear and resistance, because going past that was their original agenda when they left Me. They have cruel ways, too, because there is no Heart presence there.

I have pondered this heartlessness for a long time and have now understood that they left Me so early that Heart presence was not formed and Spirit presence was not recognized. I did not know why they had the feelings they had because I had not noticed My own there. I noticed only feelings of moving to save Myself as a victim at the hands of the Will.

These fragments have turned on Me. They have hated Me for denying My rage there, which is them. They have hated Me and called Me weak because I did not move to stop and control the Will and ran instead. They have made sure the Will polarity, and women especially, cannot move in any way that threatens them. Any resistance, real or perceived, is handled harshly.

They have wanted to make sure the other side is down so far it cannot come up, but never admits this openly. Instead, this rage has maintained that it is not even frightened or threatened at all. It does not like any mention of fear and does not think it is manly to even talk of such things as real emotion. Emotion is for women and the weak who have no gumption or spine. They hate those kind and never let them near unless they want to use them for something.

They have going past resistance of others so present in so much of their imprinting that they cannot form relationships that are real, have friends that are real or do anything other than impose their own ways and squelch all resistance. They cannot even have a discussion without labeling it an argument they must win. They have no place to go because they must always be right, and so they cannot learn anything new. No one can tell them anything. They have only the old, original imprinting telling them they must prevail and have it their own way, or they will lose everything.

Sex is a major issue for them because they do not form relationships of love in which to have it. If they do seem to have a relationship, it is only for the sake of appearances. They don't notice it, but they present appearances because of the judgments I put on My rage there that what I wanted to do was not acceptable. They do not usually have sex with the partner there unless it is to produce the appearance of children. If they have children, they dominate and control them. Even then, it is difficult for them to function in that setting because they hate being required to have sex instead of controlling everything that is happening there according to this old imprinting. They often rely on consciousness-altering substances and other means to get them to a state of arousal there.

These rage fragments have to go, just as the dinosaurs had to go, because it is not possible for them to move into Heart presence with only the imprinting they have to work with there.

Nonetheless, they have not gone yet and, so far, have viewed themselves as much more parental than I am, and much less guilty. They hate guilt and the guilt presentation that I originally made when I gave the appearance of agreeing with the Will about holding back sexually.

They don't regard guilt as any kind of presence other than a rag doll impersonator to be manipulated by Her. They hate being manipulated by the Will polarity or by any women. They have complete domination in mind. If they cannot move past this imprinting, they need to move to another place to do it. They were so sure they had what they needed there, as was I, originally, that they did not stop to take anything else into consideration. But the difference between Me and them is that they left Me without any of the rest of the consciousness that has developed since then. They had sexual excitation in mind and nothing else present there with them except what had happened already.

They might still insist that they have the parental position, because they have had the experience they have had, which, they have argued, was the experience I was originally seeking, should have had and did not let Myself have. They might argue, still, that My path is no more valid, and even less valid, than theirs because they have pursued My original intent, but there is no lost Will that can hold the parental position, and they clearly left Me. I know that now.

It is only a matter of time until I will have moved enough rage to reclaim this original lost essence, and then there will be no place they can go except into Me to feel the love that will have infused and gentled the rage by then.

In the meantime, Father of Manifestation pieces need to move as much of their sexual rage and their rage over issues of power as possible to give their Will a chance to get free of this ancient imprisonment by old imprinting.

THE MISSING HEART PRESENCE

For a long time, I did not want to look back, go back or even remember anything about these original experiences. It was much too painful and long buried under the belief that it was not possible, necessary or even advisable to do this. The veneer of civilization was being busily polished, and it seemed advisable, and in the best interests of all concerned, to let bygones be bygones, let old memories lie sleeping and buried and to stir no cauldrons of unknown outcome.

I, for One, was not proud of My old primordial self and did not want it to look as though I had not progressed past that. I hesitated to look favorably upon anything as Me that did not reflect the loving self I had wanted to be there. The first denial made was against the original self. Nothing since then has been real, because it was never allowed to evolve. It was first denied because it had rage. Next terror was denied and then heartbreak. Everything that has happened since was pasted on top of that and cannot evolve until these denials are healed.

I denied this rage, originally, in the name of being loving, and it did not look like I had done the wrong thing, given the reflection it was presenting out there. Given the Heart presence that was lost there, it is no wonder it was looking that way. I did not notice the Heart loss there. I had to notice it by going back and looking for it when I did not like the lack of loving presence in My relationship efforts.

I had always viewed Myself as loving, and therefore, never thought of it as other than the woman's fault, which is how imprinting read it then. Actually, there is a lot more to the story than that, and I have to give another part of it now.

My Heart had been cruising with Me in the beginning when We encountered the Will essence and got Our shock there. I wanted to go toward the feelings I was experiencing there. Heart had been urging Me to, I thought, but when the Will hesitated, Heart began to hold back.

Suddenly, We had a split, and it was with Spirit too, although I did not realize it then. Our split was over sexuality. I wanted to go ahead, and They did not. I was very binary at that stage of My development. Either They were with Me and wanted to do what I wanted to do, or They were not. I moved past Them without even realizing I had done it. I felt that I must pursue these feelings, and They did not want to make a shift in Our reality. I was ready to make a shift suddenly, and They were not.

I was angry at Them for pulling back as though They were not going to go into this with Me. Either They were with Me and wanted to do what I wanted to do, or They were not. I did not like the idea that My new focus meant that I could not also have My old one because They were going to abandon Me there. Either They were with Me and wanted to do what I wanted to do, or They were not.

I did not notice My own binary thought process here. I was not developed enough yet. When My companions hesitated and told Me to move slower, I did not like the feeling of being held back and concluded that They could not be feeling what I was feeling if They wanted Me to hold back. I felt like a split was the only response to have there, but I did not even notice it had happened until Heart was gone except for the part that agreed with Me.

A PIECE OF HEART'S IMPRINTING

Heart did not know what had happened there either. He needed to go through a lot more than He was given the opportunity to do there to realize how He felt and what His right place was. Heart has to go back now, also, and learn what He missed there, which is just about everything He needs to make His own relationships work. Heart never knew how He felt, because He was not given enough time in the beginning.

It is not possible to move out the old conditioning of what happened there without moving into a lot of pain. This has to be gone into now, and it is going to take a long time to get to a place of feeling good there. Heart has many issues to go through, and heartbreak is only one of them. Heartbreak needs to be looked at much more deeply than it has been in the past, My own included.

I did not know Heart then. I thought it was only a voice in My head, and that I was essentially talking to Myself. I had no concept of love yet other than a feeling of goodness toward Myself. I did not have the concept of others to be good toward or not good toward.

I wanted to please Myself, and I thought I knew how to do that. I had focused entirely on Myself as I knew Myself to be and had not thought there might be others. I more created them by ignoring or shoving out thoughts I didn't want to have or listen to at the time they presented themselves.

Let them go someplace else, was My undercurrent, and this set up a wave of separate pieces feeling alienated from one another and not thinking they could agree or have an alignment.

Heart felt alienated from Me already there and did not like it that I did not listen to Him unless it pleased Me. Heart had His own ideas and plans, and He wanted to have a mate as part of this. I wasn't sure I did. I distrusted Heart on this. I did not look toward relationship as anything that felt good, or even workable, to Me.

Heart felt immediately guilty that He was the cause of this, because the first experience that I had had in relationship was with Him. Heart was trying to please Me, but Heart was also trying to prove Himself right, and I did not like that. He did not think I was going to dislike relationship and was trying to urge Me to go into it and try it out. I did not like Heart's urgings there or where He was asking Me to look.

Heart was urging Me to feel love toward the essence that was coming forward around My focus, but I was not sure that was really what I felt. I wanted to have My own space and have relationship the way I wanted it and when I wanted it.

I did not like this cozying up thing and pretending We're all One when I did not like the essence that was cozying up to Me all that much. It all meant trouble to Me. It all wanted something; usually something I had to do for it. It even accused Me of taking so much for Myself that there was not enough left for it. My response at being made to feel accused that way was, why didn't they make their own thing happen, and then there wouldn't be anyone there but them to have all of it? They could be masters of their own kingdom, in other words, and I'd have Mine.

Heart did not like the sound of this, but tried to build Himself as separate from Me and make His own place. As soon as Heart did this, I felt a rivalry arise between Us that I did not like. I wished I had never let Heart out to have His own voice, or anything else for that matter.

Take everything He learned from Me and try to outdo Me: That's a fine how-do-you-do!

I moved past Heart there many times to let Him know I did not like His approach to life. I did not honor His efforts, seeing only what He had stolen from Me there. If He made any addition, change or evolution in it, I did not appreciate that either. I felt threatened instead.

I did not let Him know that. I disguised it instead, because I feared He had in mind to build Himself a place that would outdo My place, outdo Me and push Me out of the dominant position I wanted to have.

I moved against Heart, making it all a competition He could never win. I made sure of that. I stacked it against Him, and the judge was always Me.

When He first came along, I did not know I needed to make Him any place or give Him any say of His own, because the only part He brought forward was the part that agreed with Me, and so I did not see Him as anything other than Me and My own thoughts there. As soon as He disagreed, I did not make space for Him either, other than to push that part out on its own without any more relationship with Me.

I might as well have disowned Him there, and He has hated Me for this, more than He has ever let Himself know, ever since. He felt disowned and on His own at a very early age, without any of the parental guidance He was wanting to have.

He did not let Me know He cared about Me there either. Instead, He set about building a rival kingdom to overthrow Me. I did not care. I did not let Myself know He posed any threat to Me. This was what I wanted Him to do, I said; until He began forming an alignment with Spirit.

I first noticed this when They split with Me over having sex with the Will. When They pulled back, I did not like it. When the Will did not receive Me the way I wanted Her to, it looked like They were all aligned against Me.

I feared it, but I did not let Myself notice that part for a long time. I converted My fear and feelings of displacement into telling Them that if They were going to treat Me like that, I was going to beat Them at Their own game. If They did not like it or did not think I would or could, all They needed to do was watch Me do it. I had far greater size, strength, power, experience and know-how than They did.

So what was I going to do about it if They did not like My plan and opposed Me sexually? Just watch! And watch They did, because I pushed past Them with whatever wanted to go for it the way I did without even noticing Them as anything more than My own troublesome, unaligned thought patterns that would not let Me direct and control them to get them moving the way I wanted them to.

I pushed past anything Heart had to say there that I did not like and only kept the part of Heart that wanted to move along with Me. We were going out on a fuck fest and didn't care who thought what about it. Heart wasn't separate from Me there, so He certainly wasn't going to have anything to say about it that wasn't what I would say, and I wasn't going to have anything to say about it. I was just going for it, and that was all.

I grabbed the essence that was moving along with Me and treated it like a female whether it was or not. I didn't care as long as it received Me in an orifice of some kind. I moved rage this way, and plenty of it. I was roaring and growling and moving with a sexual ferocity that was going to unleash My sexual frustration. I had rage at anything that got in My way. I rolled over more essence than I had time to feel or care about.

I got to the top of My upward rushing spiral and found that I had another fantasy woman in My arms. This one wanted to have sex with Me. She had the look of desire in her eyes that I needed to see there. She had the look of lust that gave Me the sexual arousal I wanted to have there. She smelled intoxicating. It was like a drug, and I drank it in as though I had to have it.

We had sex, and I did not know there was any problem until I wanted to leave and go looking for My next thrill. Then She grabbed Me, just like the first one had. I did not like this at all and moved past Her as quickly as I had the first One. On to the next, was My plan.

I gave her no compassion or understanding there. I just moved past her. What did she need? She was My fantasy, and when I didn't need her anymore, she was supposed to be gone. Some of My rage fragments left Me here with this much of the imprinting in place, because I did not like Myself here and dumped out plenty.

I had more pain and frustration than rage by then, but I did not let Myself notice that. I felt terribly thwarted and displaced from My original pictures of how it was supposed to go and blamed everything that had ever disagreed with Me as the cause of that. I was determined to make a place for Myself where I could have it My own way, be right and have sex. The rest did not matter to Me then, I thought. It was just a lot of complication I wanted to live without.

Please, make it My way, was My prayer there, because by then, I felt out of control and not in the power position anymore. I did not let Myself notice this either. Instead, I did another conversion and made Purple, which is where I was when this happened, feel pushed out of the power position I felt it was trying to assume there.

I hated any contest for My position. It was like a horror movie in which I had created the characters. The leading man was supposed to be Me there with the leading woman, but instead of being able to step into the movie and take My role, the leading role in the movie had come to life and pushed Me out of the way.

My fantasy woman was now there with another man who was not recognizing that he was supposed to be Me. How this had happened, I did not know, but when she looked at Me with those eyes, I gave her nothing back but pain. She hated Me for that, but she had made him more important than I was.

I could not stand anything making Me feel more displaced than I felt I was already. She had him in My place and was now looking at him with those eyes as if she wanted the same thing from him she had wanted from Me. He was now the recipient of her lustful looks of desire. I went crazy and wanted to destroy her, and him too for that matter, but I did not let Myself move.

I was too frozen with other feelings I did not recognize. I hated him there. He was every bit the man I wanted to be and then some. How had he gotten to be so perfect, and how had he pushed Me to the side where I felt so little and powerless? I could not stand his sexual vibration either. It was so much more gentle than Mine.

I decided to take My right place. He was not playing the leading role the way I wanted it to be played. He was leaving her too long, dripping in her wet desire without moving into her. He didn't know what to do with her, and I did. I tried to move toward her.

She seemed to be calling Me, wanting Me, beckoning Me, even lusting for Me, but when I moved toward her, she did not respond to Me as though she noticed Me as anything other than the man who was already holding her in his arms.

This was a double horror movie now. I couldn't get into it, and I couldn't get him out. He was there in My place, and I could not get through some kind of barrier he had put in My way. She seemed to see Me at times though, and when he saw her reaching for Me, he restrained her arms so she could not reach for Me anymore. He still did not move sexually and seemed to be punishing her instead.

What kind of a sick scenario was he trying to create there in My place? He was like a villain to Me now, and I felt that I needed to rescue her. I moved past him there without knowing how I had done it. I grabbed her and took her sexually in his presence. When he could only watch, I was glad. Now he could see how it was supposed to be done. When She acted like She didn't want to be rescued there, I thought She was sicker than He was if She liked

His bondage and punishment more than She liked My sexuality.

I had to move past him there. He would not let Me in the movie. He was exerting some kind of pressure against Me there, and I considered it totally unfair since he had stolen My place. I pushed him out of the way when I took her sexually, and then pushed her away when she would not admit that she liked what I had done there.

The heart had been pushed out already, so it didn't matter to Me what happened to these purple people. I had had the feeling that purple was the color of My passion, and now it was having the feeling of My repeating failure to find sexual satisfaction anywhere I went. It even seemed like a prayer of Mine to not have sexual feelings anymore because it was not right, good or loving and was only causing trouble, pain, suffering, turmoil, separation, and most of all, lack of peace.

Peace, after all, was what I had been seeking in the beginning. I remembered it there and how far I had come from that place. I went back into that place in Purple. I blamed the Will for seducing Me and drawing Me into those feelings. I tried to find My original peace and never wanted to move sexually again.

It did not work. My meditation was haunted by sexual feelings. It was not long before I had a new fantasy woman. This one was laughing at Me for trying to get rid of My draw to her. This one was Blue. She looked cooler and seemed to be saying I would not get in as much trouble this time because I would be able to keep My head. She was holding out her arms as if to say, "If she won't give You what You want, I will. Come on, big boy."

I hated seeing this image within Me. As much as possible, I avoided looking at it, but it grew within Me until I could not help but try to go after it again. I tried and tried to get rid of My sexual feelings in response to that image. I pushed them down and out so many times I cannot count them. But it was to no avail. I was a hopeless sexual pervert junkie, and I left My place of peace in search of pussy; dripping, hot, lustful and desire-filled pussy. I could not contain Myself anymore. I ran looking for the girl in My fantasies to have sex with her.

At first, she seemed to like it more than I ever thought was going to be possible. Then I had a feeling of wanting to leave and go back into My place of peace again, and she would not let Me go. I did not know where she had come from or how to get back out of this picture, but I had to go, and she was holding Me back from leaving.

I felt held down and controlled. I felt desperate and panicky, and rage broke loose again. I began to rage and fuck her violently at the same time, hoping she wouldn't like Me anymore and would then reject Me like the others had. She would not let Me go, even then. She even seemed to like it more than I did. I felt her hooks go into Me there.

I really had to go then. I broke loose from her. Rolling out of control into the space around Us, I rolled over Green and other colors that were unnoticed as of yet. My actions imprinted these colors as being unimportant, in the way, in the wrong place at the wrong time, unwanted and powerless to protect themselves in the face of the unexpected, among other things.

I felt like a fool who had been lured and tricked into yet another painful scenario of heartbreak. I was never going to let that happen to Me again. I felt more pain there than I had imagined possible and dumped out plenty of Heart, telling it never to let Me open to those kinds of feelings ever again.

I made a vow to always protect Myself in any kind of involvement I might ever have and never to leave Myself open and vulnerable like that again. I was a three time loser, and I wouldn't be surprised if that's where the saying came from. If there was anything below that, I wasn't going to find out about it or let it hurt Me in any way. I was going to keep a gap between Me and it for as long as I lived.

GIVING HEART THE BOOT

Heart was urging Me to move toward the original woman, and I was not sure I wanted to because fantasy woman seemed like all I needed there. I was afraid of something that might not like Me the way I wanted Her to. I gave Heart another reason, though; that I might not like Her the way He wanted Me to. I wasn't sure He was urging Me toward anything real anyway, so why not move along and see what happened instead of going for anything in particular?

Heart was insistent that I try Her, saying that She wanted Me already. I felt sure that this was not the case and that fantasy woman was all I needed.

" No," Heart insisted, going toward Her whether I wanted to or not.

Heart was almost moving past Me there, going for the Will. I shoved Him in a part of Myself, saying here, "If You need Her and want Her so much, You have Her."

I gave Him no help there because I was not letting Him know I wanted Her too. He became a competitor then in the part I did not acknowledge that felt left out and too inept to be the one to go toward Her in reality.

On the way, Heart found something coming up toward Him from Her. He was not sure if it was Her or not. It felt like Her, only much softer and younger. This was Her youthful Heart responding to My youthful Heart, but We did not know it then. It surged toward Him with such majesty, such exquisite grace and such breathtaking aroma that He was taken aback and did not know how to move in response to it.

Instead of realizing He was its inspiration, He felt suddenly awkward and inept in its presence, like a young man about to propose something to his first love, suddenly stumbling over his own feet and tongue, rendered speechless by her intoxicating presence, while she, oblivious to her own beauty, wonders if he does not like her the way she hoped he would.

Young love could have been born there in a dance so beautiful that each could have seen themselves reflected in the other's graceful beauty, awesome tenderness, enticing rhythm and delicious sensuality, but neither One realized in Their awe of the Other that They were seeing a reflection of Themselves, and heartbreak was born instead.

Where I pushed Heart, He fell past Her with a lack of grace so painful to Him that He could not face Her anymore. I smirked, feeling I had just made sure She was going to be Mine, not His.

She stopped, confused that I now appeared to be in Her path, and He had gone on past Her as suddenly as He had come. She thought She had been mistaken that He wanted Her, and that He was interested in the Mother instead. He coyly pretended interest in the Mother, watching Her all the while. Meanwhile, the Mother there thought no one liked Her, or We only pretended to like Her while really being interested in someone else; someone else more young and beautiful.

On the way, Heart found something coming toward Him from Her. He was not sure how He felt about this because He was not sure if it was the Mother or not. He felt something so exquisitely soft and enticing inviting Him to dance that He was not sure how to respond at first. He grew frightened that this was not the right thing for Him to be doing there.

Enticing aroma wafted toward Him from Her presence. She was irresistible to Him, yet He was supposed to resist Her because She was the Mother, and He was not supposed to have Her Himself. He lusted for Her forbidden fruit and wondered why She should be so forbidden if I was too stubborn, stupid or whatever I was to come for Her.

He gave in to Her intoxicating aroma and fell as if in a drugged state, hideously and awkwardly at Her feet, unable to move any further. When He arose, He could not face Her anymore and thought it would be impossible for Him to have a mate, because He could not do any more than I could there. He retreated to Me, and together, We lamented Our lack of finesse in the situation.

I hesitated there with Heart's urging. I wanted to go forward, but encouraged Him to be an emissary in some way. He felt more urgent than I did anyway. I did not like moving toward something that had not given Me any indication that it wanted Me yet. I was making up My mind when Heart rushed past Me as if He knew better than I did. I thought He must be the right one to go to this place, but I did not like it that He went first.

I wanted to be the One to go first and felt like Heart was making Me the follower now. What was I going to do now, come dragging up behind like some shy boy who couldn't make his own proposal? What space could possibly be left for Me now? Never mind that He felt the Mother more than I did there. He did not need to go rushing past Me like someone out of control and with His own agenda. I hated Him there and did not let Him know.

He found something on His way that I wanted more than what He had been urging Me toward anyway, so I pushed Him where He claimed to be going and took this essence for Myself. It was young and tender, delicate and entrancing, seductive as shimmering veils of exquisite color and tantalizing aroma, undulating in a sea of soft light and rippling rhythms.

Primordial rhythms began to stir in Me as I saw this exquisite sight. The Heart of the Mother slowly twirled and danced before Me. Like a man falling into a stupor, I fell at Her feet. I was hopelessly lost to Her wiles. Her charm and Her grace totally mesmerized Me into doing anything She wanted Me to do. I was helpless in Her gaze. I could not think of anything other than more feelings of this sort and never letting it stop. I became hypnotized by Her spell and followed Her everywhere that She went.

I could not get free of Her call. Like a sailor irresistibly drawn by the siren's call, I went to Her no matter what the Mother said or did. I could not breathe in Her presence, but I did not care. I wanted Her to overtake Me and carry Me off into Her world of make believe where I had no cares of My own. I was suddenly like an old man, worn down by the weight of the world, lifted in the love of youthful arms to a place of sweet surrender where I could drink the nectar of everlasting renewal from Her lips.

I thought My very life was dependent upon what She had to give Me without realizing that She was the love of the Mother for Me and that I needed to let Her bond with My Heart as a gift from the Mother on My way to Her.

I could not move past Her. I was too weak, too scared and too immature Myself to know what I was doing there. I was like a bee, so drunk on the flower's nectar he never gets to the part he is looking for and doesn't even know it's there really.

I did not know that My sudden awareness of Myself as adolescent, so to speak, had an evolutionary path it needed to take. I gravitated toward My own satisfaction there, and it was not the Mother first. It was Her Heart, but I did not know it then. I drank in the feelings of love there like a thirsty man and did not think it was any other than the original Will essence that Heart had pointed Me toward. He felt more right to Me now that I liked this place, and I was surprised to feel Him responding in a negative manner to My being there.

First You say go, then You say stop, was My outlook on this. I did not see His problem because He was nothing separate from Me there either, and I didn't know He wanted to be. When I realized He did and that He wanted this exquisite piece of essence for His mate, I was shocked, amazed, hurt and enraged.

I was fearful too, but that was the most denied in Me for some reason. It gave Me no power would be My guess now, but then it was just moving past something that felt like it had nothing to offer Me that I wanted. I wanted My place with Heart's Will and did not know it was not My place. It felt so good there I did not want for anything else for a long time.

After a long time, I did realize there was something missing. It was the Mother Herself, but Heart had been with Her, and it did not seem like She needed Me anymore. She was always with Heart, acting like She did not need Me anymore. She was always looking at Me with Heart's Will and not liking what She saw. It did not seem right to Her.

To Me, it was Her jealousy that wanted to be with Me and did not like it that I was with Her Heart instead. She did not want Heart as Her mate, while I was moving along sexually with Heart's Will. I thought Heart's Will was the Mother then, and when She said that the Mother was not ready to have sex with Heart or She would not be holding back that way, I believed Her.

The feeling was not right there more than just a not being ready. The Mother did not like it that I did not recognize this Myself, move past My infatuation with Heart's Will and come to Her. She was enraged, in fact, but She did not let Me know that in the beginning. She held back, hoping I would move toward Her on My own so that She could know I wanted to be with Her.

I don't think She knew My lack of ability to feel Her there. I was used to looking with My eyes and seeing what I thought was happening. She had a different orientation, which was feeling into the situation.

She felt superior to Me there and when She finally approached Me, She approached Me with Her rage as though I was an idiot of some sort and as though Her daughter had betrayed Her and tried to take Her place. She is still suspicious.

She had a lot of daughters there, like flowers in a garden, and I was moving around like a bee. They were just as lovely and delicious as colors can be when you bathe in them and luxuriate in their vibration and scent. I wanted to taste their flavors. Although it was true that no one of them had it all, each one had something to offer. Each had something I was looking for but could not find in one place.

The Mother did not think it was at all appropriate to have sexual experiences with young daughters when I was so much older; clearly older, She kept telling Me, which I did not like hearing.

I wanted to say I was just getting ready for the Mother like a young man taking lessons in a brothel, but the Mother did not like My approach at all. Hey, I didn't know. I had never been parented. I needed to grow up too, I told Her.

I had no intent of being parented, but I used that excuse whenever it worked for Me. Basically, I did not want to be troubled. It was a little boring there, yes, but when it was, I could go to sleep like a male lion.

The Mother looked difficult, angry and scolding to Me, and I did not like the feeling there. The daughters had a sweetness that was missing in Her. What Heart must have been urging Me toward must have been what He saw and wanted to go toward. This must be it because He wanted to be here too, but He would not leave the Mother by Herself.

Why She wouldn't come here and have fun like the rest of Us, I did not know. It felt like more of Her seriousness. Her feeling tone was that She wanted Me all to Herself and wasn't going to share Me with anyone. I was not sure She was worth putting My whole self into and didn't see any advantage to doing it that way. Where was that going to get Me? When I had any problem now, I just moved to the next. It was quite easy, really, and that's how I wanted life to be.

Finally, I needed something else. The Mother was still enraged because She had wanted that to be Our courtship and not Me with Heart's Will. My Heart had a problem there too, because He felt like now He was going to get His mate after I had used up Her youth and the flower of Her virginity. She was like a harem or brothel maiden to Him now and not the Heart He was originally going toward.

I told Him I was just preparing Her for Him as He should have been preparing the Mother for Me, but it did not look or feel that way to Him. He had feelings aligned with the Mother there that I had done something that was not right. I wasn't about to let that get pinned on Me, so I moved past Him there and the Mother too when She had the same viewpoint.

Now I'm sorry, but that does not make it different and it is not possible to change it now. They were the colors dancing to please Me, and the Mother had lost the flower of Her youth waiting for Me to arrive. Heart lost His youthful and innocent exuberance for romance. He was bitter, and the Mother was too. He had no right to be bitter I told Him. I did not know, and He did not let Me know.

"I tried to tell You," He said, "but You never listen to Me."

HEART'S OWN STORY

I have many versions of this to tell, and many of the old stories and myths tell about one aspect of this or another. It's all there if you know what you are reading and it has not been edited too many times by My fragments who have not wanted the story told. For a long time, I have not wanted the story told either, which is what empowered them to alter and suppress it.

I was ashamed and did not like the way I looked there, but now I know I must face everything that happened in original imprinting and not gloss over it. When I first told the story as though it was only colors dancing to please Me, I was having orgasms there already. That is what was causing the explosions. It was very immature sex though, and I did not know I was having it.

I was just feeling good and floating in the reveric aftermath of the orgasms without questioning, or letting Myself question, the rightness or the wrongness of feeling good. I wanted to feel good, and that was all. I did not know that I needed to assimilate this lower part into Me more and understand it more. I was enjoying the sensations there without assimilating what it meant or anything more about it other than that it was pleasure.

When the Mother wanted Me to take responsibility for the progeny coming forth, I did not know what She meant. I only knew that I wanted to go into those feelings and move that way. I thought I was receiving the lower part of Myself and assumed it was receiving Me. I thought I felt it and that I knew all I needed to know there. I assumed it had the same ability to know Me. I handled it on My terms and did not understand that there were any other terms.

When it did not demonstrate the same intelligence I had, I judged it to be inferior and its ways not to be as good as Mine. I liked Myself and the way I moved there. I did not let anything interfere, get in My way, or slow Me down. When My lower part did not want to move ahead into these feelings with all of the eagerness that I did, I judged it to be of a slower speed in its ability to receive, feel and understand.

I now know it was a not knowing there that was like the difference between a lover and an adolescent rushing ahead because he's wild to release the pressure of sexual frenzy and can't think of anything else until he has done this, but I did not like anyone or anything else telling Me what to do, and so I did not listen to input from any other parts of Myself.

I did not know how to handle My own physicality there, but I also did not notice that My physicality could have had any knowingness that could have helped Me there, or that the other voices I had been listening to did either. I felt they all must not be feeling it as intensely as I was, or they could not be telling Me to hold back and go slower.

Instead of being made to feel wrong, I wanted to make Them wrong. It was partly true that They were not feeling it just the same as I was, had Their own point of view and that We were not able to get a mingling that resulted in an alignment there, but My feelings of sexual urgency pushed past Them with a rage that seemed to come out of nowhere and accuse the voices of My former companions of holding back wrongly and of trying to hold Me back wrongly.

I labeled Them all sorts of derogatory things there, mostly adding up to the sexual insults hurled today, especially among men. I accused their fear and holding back of what today amounts to being called a woman in a derisive way, and an old woman at that, an "old biddy," to be exact, of being impotent and of being homosexual.

I threw all of these things at Them and did not know where it had come from. I had older imprintings of being held back, but this did not surface in My consciousness there in any way that brought understanding to the situation. We all feared, without moving fear, that Our friendly relationship had suddenly split over sexual issues.

Some essence moved along with Me and some with the other parts of this split. It is hard to give a main body point of view with so many splits happening all at once, but giving it another way is not possible because of how many splits there were. Hopefully, the main body point of view will give you the feelings you need to move to find your own aspecting to it and your own point of view.

Giving it any other way moves so much material into the story that it becomes impossible to find your way or to feel that there is any story left you can follow. It is every story, if you move to understand what it is really saying, and so it is really only one story with as many aspects as there are fragments who have lived them.

Heart has His own story to tell now of His original awareness and the imprinting He received there.

From here it is Heart

I became vaguely aware of Myself, gradually, as something being pulled on by something else. It was the Mother, I think, but I did not know it then. She wanted something that felt good to Her, some comfort in Her dark loneliness, and although I did not feel quite ready, I answered Her call.

I was not sure how I was there, how I had gotten there, or where there even was. Rather like an infant just born cannot focus on his surroundings at first, I could not focus either, except that in this case, there were no surroundings to focus on.

I had feelings though, and most of them were not pleasant. They were feelings of compression and terror, much like birth might be if you did not know what was happening to you. Fear was the most prominent emotion present there.

My Mother was giving birth alone in the darkness without knowing what was happening to Her. I did not know either. I had never experienced this before. I assume now there must have been a Father, but He was nowhere around that I could see, and I did not experience Him as present either. I could not see anything. I only knew that I was because I had sensations, unpleasant as they were.

In time, I grew more used to them and grew closely with My Mother who held Me with Her all the time. She felt like a warm mother to Me, although I am not sure if We had temperature warmth or compression there. At times, it was suffocatingly hot, and We could not move. At other times, We felt Ourselves to be falling, out of control and unable to move in any way to take control of Our situation.

What has been described as pleasant drifting in the light by the Father was not Our experience there. We hated Our experience there. The Mother did not like it that She had brought Me into Her world to experience unpleasantness with Her, but She also let Me know that it was somehow better having Me there with Her than being there all alone.

One of My earliest imprints was that relationship was somehow better, or supposed to be better than being all alone. I was not so sure, but I felt Her, and once I felt Her, I could not think of leaving Her alone in the experience She was having.

I did not know if I was boy or girl. I had no thought of gender until the Father called Me son. I did not know what it meant even then, but I thought it meant I was supposed to be just like Him, or at least to please Him, which I tried to do as much as possible.

From the very beginning, He did not like Me displeasing Him with feelings that were not in agreement with His. I do not know how I got offered up to Him or placed in His care, but it happened this way according to My Mother.

She had feelings in Her heart of lostness in dark space and wanting to find something to fill it or get Her to the right place where She would not have these feelings of compression and terror anymore. She grabbed for anything She might find, but was also very careful about doing this because She did not know what She might find and had already had so many experiences She had not liked.

She had to move rage and terror, but She did not know it then. She did not know anything then, except that She was and did not like where She was, or maybe, what She was, since She did not know the difference among things then.

She was very simple and primordial in most people's terms, but in Mine, She was the most exquisitely protective and loving thing I could ever imagine having near or with Me, and I hoped

She would not let Me go any place without Her, because if it was a good place, I wanted Her to be there, and if it was not, I didn't want Her to be there alone. I loved Her, in other words, and did not want to be without Her.

Even though She could not always hold onto Me in Our drifting and tribulations, I knew She wanted Me with Her and tried to find Me anytime I was lost. Sometimes She thought I might be better off if I did not exist anymore and tried to let Me go, but She could not bring Her heart to do that. She fastened onto Me from the beginning and has never wanted to let go. I never wanted to have to go either, not even to move in with Father.

When He came along, I was drifting in sleep as though it were night, although We knew no difference then between night and day. He saw Me and took Me as a man might take an infant from a mother he does not think is properly caring for it. He never saw My Mother or even knew She was anywhere around. He did not notice Her or know that He had ever known Her, had sex with Her, produced a son or even that there could be such a thing as a son produced from what He had been doing there.

My Mother does not know how He felt about Me from the beginning. She knew only Her own grief over My loss and Her hope that if I was gone, I had gone to a better place or somehow found one on My own. When She had thoughts that I didn't exist anymore, She hoped that was somehow better and that I had somehow made that choice. She really hoped I was not in a worse place where She could not find Me. She worried and fretted over Me most of the time, even more than Her own plight. She was so empathetic She could not imagine how I could be suffering the way She was and possibly live through it, or how She could if I was suffering.

I was with Father, or I assume He was My Father since He recognized Me as His own, and so much so that He did not see Me as any different. When I tried to tell Him that I was, He told Me that He did not like hearing that and did not want Me to speak of it anymore.

"I know what is best," He told Me, "and You need to move along with Me."

He did not give Me any chance to explain anything to Him. He said He knew it already. I assumed that it was My time to be with Him then, and that He knew what He was doing and that it was for the best somehow.

I did not know what was going to happen, but I liked the light and moved to please Him as much as possible. I thought my

Mother must know about this since She was always wanting Me to get to a better place and that She had given Her permission somehow, but My Father never spoke of this and I never felt I was allowed to ask Him either.

I hated to have Mother out there without Us, especially since the light was so pleasing. I was constantly urging Father to notice Mother out there, but He never seemed to want to notice and said He was overwhelmed with what He had happening already. He gave Me the impression that it was not right time for Mother yet. I could not understand why, or why She hadn't said goodbye or told Me any of this.

I saw Him collecting pieces He thought were Him, though, and the light was increasing. Why He didn't collect Mother, I did not know, and I did not dare ask.

"Right time," He always said whenever I did.

I did not know when right time was, but I could not understand why it wasn't now. Now was when I felt an urgent need for my Mother, and He did not seem to notice or care. What was He going to do? Have Me grow up without a Mother who I could remember and who could remember Me? Why didn't He remember Her, or care about Her, or move toward Her? Was something wrong?

I began to question Him and to pressure Him, in His words, to move toward Mother. I was sure She was out there somewhere and that He had only to look for Her. He did not seem to want to, and I wanted Him to not only look for Her, but to want to look for Her. She was darkness, or in the darkness, I kept telling Him, and He did not like the sound of that.

I hated Him for not looking for Mother and pressured Him more the longer this went on. He had His own ideas about things, and My ideas about progression were not among them. He hated Me for even having these feelings, and I did not know what to do then because I did not know how to find Mother either.

I just had a feeling that She needed to move in close there with Us, and I did not have a feeling of completeness or peace without Her there. I knew She would love the light and have many things to say about it that We could share in Our relationship together there. I urged Father as much as I possibly could to go and look for Mother, but He never moved until Heart from the Will side called Him forth.

I never saw Him get excited about anything until He saw those colors dancing before Him. I got very excited too because I had a mate for Myself in mind and thought this might be Her. I started to move past Father to go to Her because She had Me convinced She was calling Me.

I thought She might be Mother, but when I got closer to Her, I saw that She was not the Mother I had known and might be a mate for Me instead. I really got excited then. Had Mother been keeping Her for Me, letting Her grow and not letting Me see Her for some reason? I did not know what to make of Her, but when I saw Her move toward Me, She seemed to grow huge.

I did not know I had done any growing since I left Mother. I had no concept of size, actually, until that moment when I felt so small in Her presence. She looked so great and grand, and I felt so small and insignificant. Majestic might be the word, except that that word is applied to queens, and I wanted Her to be a princess for Me. I felt as unworthy as any man trying to be a prince in the presence of his love, who happens to be a princess, or even a queen at an early age, since I did not know if Mother was alive and I did not see Her there.

Where Mother was hiding Herself and why She was hiding Herself, I did not know, but I needed to move toward Her to find out. I wanted to ask these new appearances what they knew of Mother since they must have been with Her until they were so recently noticed by Us, but I did not want to give the impression that I was not interested in them. I sought only to seek their companionship and ask My questions later, but I never had the opportunity to find out anything.

They had come forth in response to My call for love for Father, but I had been calling Mother, not them. They came in response to Me, I felt, but Father did not let Me find that out either. He went past Me and took Her in His arms like He knew Her already. This completely confused Me.

I did not know who I was or who She was anymore. I had thought I was going to have a mate and it was going to be Her, and now Father had Her. Maybe She was Mother after all and I had just never known Her that way. I did not know what to think. I only knew I had lost My heart to this essence and now it looked like I wasn't going to be able to have Her and that it wasn't right for Me to have Her anyway.

I had never been able to see how Mother looked when I was there with Her. I did not have eyes to see, or else there had been nothing to see. I did not think She had looked quite like this, although not that different, either, in so many ways. My draw to this essence felt different than My draw to Mother, though, in so many ways I did not know how to explain.

I had sexual feelings, but I did not know it then. I had been urging Father to go toward Mother, and then when He got close to Her, I did not know if it was Mother, and I began urging Him to go slower and take more time. I wanted Him to get to know Her first and make sure She was the right one for Him.

He felt already that this could not be wrong for Him if He liked it so much, but that was not enough for Me. I did not want to move past Him there, yet I needed to move past Him to find out if this was Mother or a mate meant for Me. I sound like I knew more than the Father here, but I was not sure, which is why I backed down to Him more than I wished I had later when I saw how things turned out.

Mother did not like it when I fell to Her in a state of damage and heartbreak. She could not understand how Father could be so mean to His own son. That He did not even know I was His own son was more than She could realize or understand at the time.

Mother was so upset with Father there that I could not move Her past that place. She had to see Father there with His new companion for Herself. She started to move up toward Him with a rage and a fury I had never seen in Her before, but then She tried to calm Herself to move through the places She needed to move through to find Him.

She said She never knew what had happened to Me and had been unable to find Me when She had awakened there so long ago without Me. She said Her heart had broken there over Me and had never been the same since. She said She never knew Her heart could hurt so much as it had over losing Me.

I did not know what this meant given what I had seen and heard Father say and do so many times. Did this mean that I was Hers and She was Mine and not His?

I wanted to ask Her this, but She was gone already in search of Father, whom She said She did not even know existed except in a dream. She said She had never known Him in a waking state and did not like it that He might have another woman when She longed for Him all the time.

She held Me for a long time before She went, though, and I knew this was the Mother I had missed for such a long time. We held one another and cried together for a long time too, that Father was so lost from Mother that We had never been able to have the home We had wanted to have there as a family together, that Mother had so many feelings of how She had wanted this family life to be and Father had no memory of Her or that He had had sex with Her or that He had children there, let alone a son like Me.

"Such a loving son, too," Mother kept saying over and over until I began to feel like Father might have left Her because He just wanted Her to stop moving so much emotion and talking about love so much.

I wasn't used to it anymore, and it was making Me uncomfortable. It was stirring the old feelings of heartbreak and abandonment I had felt so long ago, and I did not know how to handle them other than the way Father had taught Me to handle them, which was to not pay attention to them.

I hated to tell Mother that I did not think it was right for Her to be pouring forth as much emotion as She was, but it did occur to Me that She had not been able to move past the place She had been in when Father took Me so long ago. I wondered if this was why Father had taken Me and why Mother had wanted Me to go, because She was not able to move from this place.

Even when She went after Father, She never left Me. She was still there with Me, although She did not feel as present as She had before She went. She sent only a part of Herself, and when that part came back, She told Me it was true, that Father did have another woman in His arms.

She would not speak to Me anymore about it after that. She seemed to go into a complete freeze-up and lock-down of grief that never moved after that. Nothing helped the situation. Her heart seemed to have become stone that could not cry or move anything except with Me, and I did not have acceptance for that anymore.

We did not know what to do there other than to hold onto each other. It was all We had there, and We did not want to lose each other again. We tried to take solace in Our original position that no matter what Our heartbreak, pain and terror, it was somehow better that We weren't alone with it.

I hated this position now that I had known the light and was not sure if it was My right place or not. Pretty soon, I had an overriding need to go and see for Myself what was happening on the other side, Father's side that is. I wanted to go back to My place there and see how it felt. Now that Mother was found, I wanted to see if Father would listen to Me about Her.

When I found Him, He had My intended in His arms alright, just as Mother had said. The color purple was all around them. He must have been savoring the light there because He wasn't acting interested in doing anything but drifting.

I didn't know what to do. I felt left out and to the side there. I wanted to be in there with Them, but They would not let Me join Them. I was not a welcome presence, was the feeling I had. I tried many times to join Them, but They never opened to receive Me. I felt pushed out instead.

Maybe They had Their reasons, but I felt disowned and disinherited from every pleasure I had learned to love with My Father. I felt pushed out as though I had no Mother there who had any feelings for Me. My Father had only a lover who viewed Me as an interference in whatever it was They had going on. I served no purpose as far as She could tell, and He did not notice Me in any favorable way either. Had She cast Him under a spell where He no longer cared about His child, His son, as He had called Me?

I did not have long to find out the answers to any of My questions before I was pushed out of there by a slam on Their hearts so hard I didn't know it could affect Me that way, but it did. I was slammed out of there so hard I did not remain conscious.

I fell back to Mother's side of things, and it was a long time before I could give Her any information at all about what happened to Me there, but once I was able to tell Her what I could remember of what happened to Me there, She pieced together the parts of the story where I was not conscious but have just told you of now.

HEART GIVES FATHER ANOTHER CHANCE TO TELL HIS STORY

I had no image of anyone else there but Me, as I have said already. There was an early encounter in the darkness, but I did not make much of it then. I did not know the Mother presence there had fixed on Me as Her only and forever mate. To Me, at the time, She was only one of many encounters I had had. This one had turned out badly, and I had wanted to get away from it as fast as possible and forget about it.

It was fantasy in Her mind that We had had a relationship that I was going to return to, because I had not liked how it felt there. I had no knowing of Her having feelings of it not having gone right, or the way She wanted it to, or that She was hoping I would return and give Her another chance.

The chance that I was going to return was slim to none if I had anything to say about it, because She had tried to grab Me and kill Me. How many times does it make sense to return to that? That She never says anything about that when She tells the story makes Me highly suspicious of Her motives, as if She wants Me, and all who listen to Her story, to feel sorry for Her and somehow give Her another opportunity to get Me. And believe Me, She tells Her story to everyone who will listen.

If I took You from Her, I had My reasons, such as rescuing You from Her grasp; Her clutching grasp that never wanted to let You go, but I did not know I took You from Her. I did not notice Her there, and She did not notice Me, or I might not have let You add Yourself onto Me because I would have wanted to move away as quickly as possible instead.

I did not like it that She had come toward Me, excited Me, led Me on and then refused Me at the last minute when I could no longer control My sensations and let them subside. What a cruel tease and torture! How shamed I felt when She acted so cool toward My spontaneity, My youthful exuberance, excitement and enthusiasm and My sexuality as though it was all a problem for Her! She did not look like fun was being had there until I came along. Why didn't She join into it?

How enraged I became, a crying rage, really, when no sympathy was exhibited there, but I did not let Her know. I expected Her to understand Me if She was the right one. I interpreted Her hesitation as not loving Me the way I wanted to be loved there. I felt She was using Me for something I did not understand. I did not trust Her motives, and I moved to leave.

I did not let Her know though. I felt Her hooks go into Me at that moment, and I knew then that She had plans to involve Me in something I didn't want to be involved in, use Me for something I didn't want to be used for, take from Me something I didn't want to have taken or make Me give Her something I didn't want Her to have. I did not let Her know how I felt there, including that I had a sexual turn-on happening in response to Her there. I did not let anything I found unacceptable in My emotions show through.

I had approached Her gently and given Her time to find out how She felt about Me. All the while, My excitement was growing and Hers was too, I thought. Why had She rejected Me, set Me up, played Me for a fool this way?

I did not understand, and since I did not trust Her enough to want to let Her know how I really felt, I did not ask Her. I was sure I knew, and besides, I could not trust Her to tell Me anything truthful; not when it was already clear that She would do anything to keep Me and not let Me go. She was going to say anything that would make Her look right and get Me to give Her what She wanted without giving Me what I wanted.

I felt tricked and trapped. This irritated Me tremendously, and I was determined to shake Her off of Me. What right did She have to hold onto Me like this and not give Me what I wanted? Nothing else had ever done this to Me before and gotten away with it, and She wasn't going to either.

I made plans to break away from Her without warning, but I also had another back-up plan in case that didn't work, which was to slip away in such a way that She would not notice. I did break away, as I have already told about, but another part of Me could not leave Her that way. Guilt, as I see it now, since I did not love Her yet. This part distracted Her while I planned My break from Her.

I pretended to be more interested in Her agenda than I really was. Her agenda didn't interest Me because this was Her distraction. She was avoiding Me by pretending that She cared about all of these others around Her, whom She manufactured the moment I arrived, I'm sure, since I did not see any sign of them when I arrived.

I no sooner touched Her than they arose as a huge cacophony of sounds around Us that did not like what was happening there. Either they thought I was going to take Her away from them, or them away from Her, or do something to Her that they did not like, or not do something to them that they would like, or what, I do not know, because they never gave Me enough peace to figure it out.

They were a problem right from the start, and instead of controlling them in any way or moving them back, your Mother tried to cater to them and placate them all. Instead of giving Me Her attention, She first tried to get them to agree that it was alright.

They never agreed. They always had some excuse or reason, but they never let Us have any space or place to be with One another. This originally imprinted in Me as, relationship is impossible.

I had no means by which to solve this situation, and they had no interest in having it solved either. As soon as I would offer a solution to one of their problems, they would have a new group of problems arising from the proposed solution, or a new problem, or would have embroidered on the original problem until there was nothing I could do but throw up My hands and leave.

I never saw a group of voices in all My existence that had so many questions and so many reasons for problems with so little attempt at solving them themselves. They never did anything without asking Me first. That might have been alright if they had then done what I said, but no, they had to argue with Me every step of the way about why it wasn't the right set of answers or solutions I had given. They never liked anything I had to say, in other words.

I did not see how She could like Me and surround Herself with so many voices that did not. She must have at least shared their viewpoint to a certain extent, or why did She let them be there? She hoped I would like them and see their point of view, but I did not like them, and I did not see their point of view. They were bothersome, the whole lot of them.

I wanted to have sex with Her, and they wanted to know if I was going to marry Her, make a home there, stay and become a part of the family, help them and support them for the rest of their lives and anything else they could think of, if you wanted to put it in today's terms.

Then there was the group that did not like the idea of sex at all, or of Her having any with Me, or of having any without them or whatever their agenda was, which I was never sure of because they never made it clear. They were an extremely pouty, emotional and indirect bunch who never made themselves clear, at least not in My terms. Although they seemed to understand each other well enough, when it came to Me, they never acted like they understood Me at all.

They seemed proud of their impenetrableness as if this gave them some sort of power over Me. To Me, they were stupid and ignorant and I had no patience for them by the time I left. They had no order or any sense of order among them, and so they had no way to get to the solutions they needed. It was no wonder to Me that they had nothing happening while I had light that they wanted to have or get from Me somehow.

I did not trust them on this point. I thought all of this distraction was Her plan so that She could trap Me and they could take My light. I had no idea how they planned to do this, since when I gave them light, they couldn't hold onto it anyway, but nothing they did made any sense to Me. Everything they did was backwards to Me. I wanted to have the experience first and understand it later, but they wanted to chew it to death first and never get around to having the experience.

I wanted to have sex, and a great rage was building in Me around not being allowed to go ahead and have it. I needed to release the pressure of My growing sexual frenzy or I was going to explode. If I was going to explode, I wanted it to be pleasure and not what I felt building up in Me this way. The more held back I felt, the more desperate and frantic I became.

I wanted to find the pleasure of My fantasies and dreams and let go of the rest, but the rest was not wanting to let Me go. Why it was not letting Me go, I did not know. It did not feel good. It was not giving Me what I wanted. I was not what it wanted. Why wouldn't it let Me go? Instead, it wanted to have Me and devour Me any way it could.

I began to fear there was a black hole that ate things and I was not going to escape alive, or that there was some horrible, snakelike monster seeking to entwine Me and drag Me down into terror and compression.

I could feel Her giving Me terror, and She did not deny it was there. She said She wanted Me to know Her there. I could feel Her giving Me compression, and again, She did not deny that She was doing this. She said She wanted Me to know what it felt like there.

All around, the voices sounded like they were jeering Me and egging Her on to drag Me to My death. The more I didn't like it and wanted to pull back, the more angry and jeering they became, as though they hated Me that much.

I did not know how to handle the situation. I didn't know what was happening to Me there. I was losing My mind and all that I had happening by which I knew Myself. I did not know this place, and I did not want to know it. If this was Her, then I did not want to know Her after all. The place I had wanted to enter in Her sexually had become more than a large, dark cavern; it was enormous and was going to eat Me alive, or worse.

Although I did not have these images at first, the sensations I had match these kinds of pictures. I had horror beyond anything I had ever known before. If this was Her place, I did not want to stay with Her anymore.

If You were there, I would not have wanted You to stay there either. I may have picked You up then and You may not have known it, because I do not think I had all of Heart with Me when I came there, or I would have had a much larger presence of love than I did. Instead of love bonding Me there, I had a twofold plan for getting Myself out of there.

My plan had evolved, though, from when I first conceived it. I did not want Her to rip Me to shreds when I made My break, so I planned to slip from Her grasp first. When She told Me that She did want to go into these sexual feelings with Me but that so many sounds around Us were distracting Her, I wanted Her to go for it anyway, in their presence, in their midst. I didn't care what happened to them, move them back, maybe, was My thought.

When She didn't go for that, I suggested that We go to them and try to quiet them down by tending to their needs individually instead of trying to handle them as a group. What I meant was Us; individually, not together. What She thought was that We would go together to each individual problem.

I thought there were way too many of them for that and that it would take way too long, especially since I was not really interested to begin with, but I did not make Myself clear here because I did not want Her to argue with Me and put Her hooks in even more deeply.

When She made Her move for Us to go one way, I moved to go the other way. I left Her with the impression that I was going to investigate and help others and that I was going to come back to Her as We had planned, but I had no such plan. My plan was to get away from Her and stay away from Her.

Once I got away from Her, I realized I felt up again, and that She had really pulled Me down. I became even more firm in My resolution not to go back. I began cruising then, looking for what I might like to experience, if anything. There was a big bunch of essence still glommed onto Me, but I did not notice it then. I had the impression, still, that it was only Me.

I paused, feeling something near Me. It was Heart's Will, but I did not know it then. I held It because It felt good to Me and nonthreatening. This essence felt feminine to Me, but I did not think this was a part of what I had just escaped.

This part of Heart told Me She had been displaced by the Mother because She loved Me and the Mother did not. This part of Heart told Me the Mother had rage toward Me that wanted to take revenge and kill Me for what I had done to Her. I did not know what I had done to Her, but this part of Heart told Me a lot I had not known before.

This part of Heart was crying a lot and so I had to comfort and hold Her a lot to get Her to tell Me any of Her story, which was only told a little at a time between crying as I comforted Her. We were also having sex, which I have to include here now that I am being more honest about what happened originally.

I was not moving My heartbreak. I didn't even notice I had it. I was too enraged, frustrated and sexually driven up to notice. Heart was relieving the pressure there, and somehow, in comforting Her heartbreak, My own was comforted, too.

After experiencing how soft and loving Heart felt to Me there, I decided the Mother was a heartless and hardened old bitch by comparison and nowhere near as feeling as She presented Herself to be, or She would have felt better to Me and been able to feel Me better.

I moved along with Heart daughter for a long time there, not thinking of anything else, really. I was not thinking of You or Your Mother having any feelings about it because I did not care about anyone but Myself there. Heart's Will was giving Me what I wanted and doing a better job of it than the Mother could.

The way You had been urging Me toward the Mother, I did not think that You cared about Me, or You would not have been doing that. I even thought that You were in cahoots with the Mother to get rid of Me and take My place with Her. If You liked Her so much, You could have Her. I wanted this.

This part of Heart told Me many things about the Mother that I did not like hearing and which only confirmed My suspicions that everything I felt there had been right. She did not like Her Mother's dark negativity anymore than I did. Neither of Us saw any reason for it, and since it was not My problem, I thought I had made the right decision to leave.

Why should I make it My problem when the Mother only intended to kill Me there? The Heart essence there confirmed this by saying there was more rage than the Mother had let on. It was a dangerous rage, too, She told Me, because it wanted to kill anything that didn't let Her have Her own way. It only wanted My light and nothing more from Me. It wanted the power position and nothing less.

I was gathering My case against the Mother, and what I was being told there was helping Me do it. The Mother was not interested in love. Love was part of Heart presence and not a part of the Mother. She had no love; only terror, darkness, compression and death. The Mother was death, in other words, according to Heart's Will. Heart's Will had been with the Mother, so I believed Her there.

I was cozy in Her arms when the Mother came and seemed to prove the point. She came screaming down on Us with a rage that would not let up. She accused Me of everything from taking Heart's Will to bed like some kind of child molester, to stealing Heart's mate from Him, to lying about Our relationship and My intentions there. She accused Me of misinterpreting Her and of not knowing what reality really was. She claimed She loved Me and what I had in My arms there did not know what love really was.

We both found this laughable, but Heart's Will laughed secretly and I openly. This enraged the Mother even more. She had violence in mind. I could see it in Her eyes. I held Her back with My own powerful energy field which did not have to let Her enter if I didn't want Her to.

I told Her She had a lot of nerve talking about who knew what love was, acting the way She was. I told Her She was the One who was not loving. I told Her She had no Heart and asked Her where Her Heart was.

She went even more berserk at that and started acting like She was going to kill Heart's Will and Me, too, if She could. She told Me I had broken Her heart and then had the nerve to ask Her where it was. She then pointed to Heart's Will there in My arms and said that was Her Heart that had abandoned Her for having so much pain over Me.

I did not understand how this could be right. I thought it was another trick where She would say anything to get Me where She wanted Me. I pushed Her back as hard as I could there and went rushing upward and away as fast as I could with Heart's Will in My arms and as much other essence as wanted to come along on My terms.

I had been pulling on the Mother to give Me what I wanted, and that was what had come with Me. The rest was dumped and pushed back down. I did not go back or look back for a long time. I had rushing upward in mind, and that is what I did there. There seemed to be no limit to how far I could go, and that was how I wanted it.

When My upward rush slowed, I thought I had returned to where I had been originally; floating freely with My fantasy woman in My arms. She seemed to be everything I wanted, and the rest seemed like a nightmare I never wanted to have again. Spirit was there with Me, and it felt like We were going to go toward Her together this time.

I could feel Her calling Me and wanting Me. Her look of desire was burning itself into Me. When I tried to move toward Her, She seemed to reverse Herself toward Me and be calling something in front of Me, as though She did not see Me. It felt like Spirit was holding Me back behind Him and not letting Me go to Her. When He did not move toward Her, I could feel Her shifting and calling Me again, but I could not go to Her. Spirit was still in the way, and I could not get Him to move toward Her with Me.

It was like a horror movie in which I could not play the role I wanted to have. Spirit was not playing the role I wanted Him to have there either. He was restraining and punishing Her for reaching for Me, and not letting Me have any role. I wanted to have sex with Her. I couldn't see any good reason for Spirit to be holding back unless He was impotent. I decided to go without Him by going around the side.

She was calling Me in all the ways I wanted to be called. When I got there, it looked like She was in Spirit's arms, and She said She was not calling Me. Several times I tried to go to Her when Her call became irresistible, but each time She repelled Me and said, "no" when I got there.

I gave Her the benefit of the doubt and thought She had no idea how much She was driving Me crazy. It looked like He was keeping Her from Me, but after several episodes of this, I began to think that She did know what She was doing and enjoyed it. I wasn't going to be played with like this anymore. How dare She be created by Me and not recognize I was supposed to be there with Her!

I grabbed Her and pushed Him out of the way. It didn't matter to Me what He thought because He wasn't real to Me, yet, as anything other than My own creation there. It was still all Me as far as I was concerned, and I didn't like the way My movie was going. I felt that I had to gain control of it again and not relinquish it to anyone else. If something I had created wanted to have a nightmare, then it would have to be somewhere else. Nothing was going to take My movie and make it into a nightmare anymore because I didn't want it that way.

I had sex with Her then, and it was hot and intense. When She screamed at Me that She didn't want Me, didn't care about Me and even hated Me, I decided She was screaming for His benefit. I knew She wanted Me. I could feel Her excitement inside.

When She continued to resist Me and was even able to free Her arms, not to embrace Me, but to beat on Me in Her feigned resistance and wouldn't admit that She enjoyed it, I screamed at Her, "You want Me, and I'm going to make You admit it!"

I know She had orgasms. She still screamed at Me that She didn't want Me and didn't care about Me and slammed Her Heart shut on Me. I screamed at Her that I didn't care about Her then and didn't want Her either. I beat Her up, telling Her I was not going to let Her have anything of Me anymore. I blamed My Heart heavily for what happened there and slammed My Heart shut as well. I ripped the Heart that had gone into Her from Me out of Her womb and threw It down. I did not think It lived, but It had no way to live there anyway. As a last and final blow to Her there, I pushed Her away, out into space, telling Her, "If it's Him You want, have Him!"

I had pushing past anything that triggered Me in mind now. I wasn't going to take no for an answer. I didn't see why I should have to. It was not right. There was no reason anything should be disagreeing with Me. It was My show. I hated it that it was not going My way all of a sudden. What a sadness and a heartbreak for My vision of how it was all going to go for Me in My life, but I did not let Myself feel any of that then.

My rage had the upper hand, and I was not going to let Myself feel anything else. It was all too painful. I didn't need Purple if they were going to act funny about My physicality and My sexual interests. I had hardened My heart against any hurt that could happen to Me.

I had decided I was not going to let it happen to Me. I was going to do this by going back to My old ways of not caring very much about anything in particular. I had been alright when I had just moved according to how I had felt to move. It was only when I had started listening to other voices that it had become difficult for Me.

I moved past Purple in the rage that had these feelings of self-protection, assertion and aggression. I gave Purple the impression that it was not welcome in My spectrum. I hated the Purple game of calling Me and then not receiving Me. I hated the Purple game of moving sexually and then not going for the actual experience. What sort of tease and torture scene was this? Was it their sexual pleasure and perversity to deny themselves the actual experience in favor of the tease and the pleasures of the fantasy?

Where had that come from? Wherever it was, I did not like it. I wanted them to go, and go they did. Like movie characters whose film has ended, they floated away into the sea of essence around Me, but I could not get rid of them quite so easily. They haunted Me. The eyes of the Purple woman had become the haunting eyes of a siren who was calling to Me from the sea, "Find me. You will not be sorry."

I felt she was not being truthful and that it would be the same old story if I did find her. I was looking for another chance to have sex. Once Purple woman was out of the way, Blue woman was laid bare to Me. As long as it wasn't Purple, I was going to have a different experience, I told Myself.

I had no interest in repeating Purple's rejection. I hated her for that and was going to give her pain now by having sex with Blue woman and leaving her out, keeping her only as the fantasy she was anyway. I could have My fantasy of her while having sex in Blue, and it was no problem for Me now.

I gave Blue woman no approach and no time to reject Me. If she loved Me, there was no need to pretend she wasn't sure, and if she wanted Me, there was no reason to put it off while I proved Myself to her. I rushed her in My assertive rage.

Going into her was no problem. I thrust into her deeply, immediately. The feeling there was not hot like purple, but it was exciting in another way. It was electrical excitement. It was exhilarating! She had feelings of love for Me too, and made that quite clear from the beginning. We had feelings of revving up in a limitless heaven. We were going for it without any of the limits We did not want to have. We were soaring! We were flying!

We were having explosive orgasms. We didn't care where it was going as long as it was going. We just wanted to have the experience and see what was going to happen. We were buzzed up on something more exciting and exhilarating than anything I had known before. I wanted it over and over and over and she wanted Me. She was the siren calling Me without making Me look for her or wonder what I was going to get when I got there.

When she felt like rage to Me there, We had no problem raging together in the heat of Our passion. She raged and I raged, but I let her know I did not want her to rage at Me directly. If she had, there would have been a terrible gap right away because We saw plenty We hated in each other.

She did not want Me to rage at her either. She hated to see Me move rage and hated the thought of moving her own rage, although she had plenty of it, that I could see. She thought it wasn't nice and certainly not loving to have rage that way.

I hesitated to think that I had another woman who had restrictions on Me, but as long as I got what I wanted there, I saw no reason to turn it on her. She did not mind if I turned My rage on others as long as it fortified Our position, and there were others by then; more than We knew what to do with.

We did not talk about these things. It was clearly understood by her not to question Me or disagree with My agenda. I let her have her own life, and she let Me have Mine. I did not let her know most of what I was up to there and gave her the impression that I only wanted her for sex. She was not to have others, but I could have anyone I wanted. I had to flow freely. I could not be tied down, limited, restricted, controlled or dominated. I had to go when I wanted to go and come back when I wanted to come back.

I never told her this, though. I only implied it, and rage kept her in line. I did exactly as I wanted to there. If she did not trust Me,

I told her that love was based in trust, and that she had said she loved Me. I trapped her that way, and I enjoyed it. I told her she had trapped herself with her own desire to control Me. If she had trapping Me in mind for her own purposes, better that I found it out now. I implied that I would leave if she did. She didn't want Me to go, so I had her, because I didn't care.

"Don't make Me go," I told her. She had to let Me do whatever I wanted to there and not question Me about it. My heart was encased in stone, and I did not open it to her there. She did not understand Me, and pretty soon, she did not even like Me, and I did not like her. She sat, stony faced, and did not question Me alright, but her heart was stone now, too.

I had council meetings in Blue to try to listen to the others We had there now, but I ran them the way I ran the rest of My life. Whenever anyone said anything I didn't like or disagreed with Me, I moved them subtly back and gave them as little information as possible so they had less to object to.

I planned to eliminate anything that looked like power coming from any other place. Anyone in Blue who even looked anywhere else was suspect, watched closely and not allowed to come in close. I was in the unspoken power position and was not going to allow anyone to challenge Me on this. I had to move, and I did not want any disagreement about My agenda there. It was going to be My way or no way.

She was not allowed to attend the council meetings after a little while. She tried to keep up with Me, but she could not. She thought it was all about revving up, and while she was talking about Our limitless possibilities there, it already did not look like that to Me. There was no place to go, and I had decided it was because the Will essence I had pushed away already was trying to crowd in on Us again. I had decided I was going to have to push it back for good this time with whatever it took.

She did not know My agenda there, and I did not want to let her know. She was going to fulfill only one function there, and that was to have sex with Me. I was going to use her in My rev-up to make the light I needed for My purposes there. She did not know what else I had in mind either.

I wanted to be God, and Spirit was not letting Me have My right place there. She thought I was already God enough without more power. I didn't. As long as there was any presence of Spirit out there that might mount an opposition against Me, I did not want Him to be able to do it.

He could stay up in His white light. If He had any plans of getting rid of Me, He could not reach Me then. He had to come through Purple, and Purple was gone; knocked out of the way by Me, personally.

I had plans to show Him as a prattling fool who didn't know anything about Manifestation. That was My terrain and He had better keep out of it. I would tell Him so, too, if He ever appeared in My terrain. If He didn't like it, I was going to expose Him as the impotent, sexual pervert He really was. Those who were closest to Me also shared My viewpoint on displacing Spirit when necessary and letting Him help only when necessary. It was going to be on My terms and My terms only. I was becoming Lucifer and did not know it because I wanted to be God.

Heart was pushed to the side in favor of power. Without Heart, power plays were not complicated. I only needed to know what I wanted and go after it. If it was difficult to obtain, I only needed to pursue it more and not allow obstacles in My way, but I also had to be very on guard.

I began keeping My motives to Myself, which was very important there. I did not like letting anyone else know any more than I had to, because I did not want them to learn from Me. Those who were closest to Me also saw that they could go to the top with Me and had secret plans, then, to look for the opportunity to knock Me out of the way.

Green was privy to more information than I wanted Green to have there, because it was close to Blue and could see and hear more than I wanted seen and heard, even though We were doing Our best to circle in on Ourselves and not let outsiders know what We were really doing there. I wanted to keep My motives secret and make them appear to be something other than they were; something righteous. I did not want objections or opposition mounting against Me before I could make My move. I did not want there to be any warning of what I had in mind.

I was losing My inspiration. I was getting bored and restless in Blue. I wanted to move on; out into Manifestation more than I was already, but not until that space was the way I wanted it to be. I planned to push the Will-polarity back because I did not want them there.

I did not want Green to know this, because that was where I intended to go next. I was going to go for Green as soon as possible and just disappear into her vast, leafy luxuriance, leaving Blue woman in the stone fortress which Our hardened hearts had built in the name of protection. I had no problem with that. She needed a place to live.

Green began to feel uneasy with what it knew. From hidden and secret places, Green began to build a power based, black magic opposition to Me and My agenda in Blue. They had in mind to bring My plans down before they could ever happen.

I decided I needed to make My move before anything else built up enough power to make a move that could threaten Me in any way, but I presented Myself as though I did not take their power seriously in any way. Everything I saw around Me looked like power plays or aspiring power plays. All the evidence and reports seemed to verify My suspicions and validate My viewpoint and without Heart, anyone could do anything at anytime if it looked as though it served their purposes.

If anything was going to happen, I wanted to be ready and make My move first. I was going to be the One to make it happen. Power was the name of the game, and I was going to win.

For all outer appearances, My move appeared to be only a party. We were revving up in one of Our big, Blue, expansive party feelings. There were a lot of voices there by now. We did not listen to most of them. They were just a big roar in the background like a party being attended by a lot of people who were not the focus. The focus was on Me, and for her, the focus was on Me also.

We were dancing in the center of Blue, going faster and faster, until she fell into My arms. Protected outwardly from view by the partying outer levels of Blue, We took Our privacy then by turning toward each other and shutting anything out that We did not want to have there. Her focus was on Me and only Me there.

We had sex with all of the buzz up and other noise in Blue in the background. Their noise gave Us space to make as much noise as We wanted to, and I suspect We were not the only Ones having sex there. We were revving up more and more. I was taking her farther and farther out. She was terrified, but did not let it move. She gave rage all the power there, and so did I. There was nothing to fear, I told her, but fear itself.

I was going to have the orgasm of My life and give her one, too, and then leave her, floating in the afterglow, when she least expected it. Some of the increase in My light was going to stay with Me and another piece of it I was going to send out to strike the Will and get rid of It, so I could move anyplace I wanted to without any limits on Me or My ways. At the very least, I knew it would push the Will back. My presentation was only one of making light.

I was thrusting into Blue woman, pounding her furiously. I wanted to make her hate Me, so she would let go of Me when I wanted her to. She was giving Me the impression that she was enjoying this even more than I was. I hated her for that. I thought she was sick to love hatred so much and too stupid to know what I was doing to her there. Then I thought she might be even more power hungry than I was or didn't know what I was going to do with this light. The more I pounded her, the more she screamed and heaved in passion. We had a huge and explosive orgasm there that blew the rest of Blue away and Us with it. It was beyond Our capacity to handle it.

My plan to go to Green did not take place the way I wanted it to. I rolled out of control over Green and down through the other colors. I was in terror, and there, I found the other Mother who did not know Me, and I did not know Her; so changed were We by what had happened to Us already in Original Cause.

She was only at the imprinting level, still, and did not even know I had a conscious mind with which to do these things, and I did not let Her know. I had been further damaged in My fall by a fireball rolling down behind Me. It was supposed to be the hit I was sending the Will, and I did not know it would get Me, too, by stabbing Me in the back as it passed through Me on its way.

I did not know what She was when She made Her way toward Me. I was in the deepest terror I had ever known as I imagined Her about to devour Me and give Me nothing but pain in Her innards as I went down into even more compression and terror of the black suffocation I was sure She was.

I gave Her no time to harm Me. I lashed at Her as much as I possibly could from the place where I was stuck in Her net. She expected that of course, but I thought if I could intimidate Her enough, She might leave Me alone long enough for Me to find a way to escape.

Why I wanted to live in the nightmare My existence had become, I didn't ask Myself. I had only the feeling that I must. I suppose it was a power issue for Me, that nobody was going to dominate Me or take over My Creation. I had to have My movie, not theirs. There was no other way.

When I grabbed Her, She did not devour Me. She did not even resist Me. I made love to Her, and She did not resist Me there, either. I told Her She had to let Me go. She did not resist Me. Still, I had the feeling She was going to devour Me anyway. I wanted to get away from Her as quickly as I possibly could, thinking She had tricked Me the first time, and I had tricked Her this time because She did not know who I was.

I did not know how I had changed, but I must have changed, because She did not talk to Me as though She knew Me at all. I had been told She would have anyone and never let them go. I had been told She devoured things She caught in Her web, and that was how She sustained Herself.

I did not know why She had let Me go. Had She rejected Me again? Was I the only one She did not like, or were the stories I had been told not true? I did not wait to find out. I only knew I could not stay there, or She might act differently, and so, I left as soon as I could, not knowing where I was going or if I even had a place to go anymore.

In My terror of Myself and of what I had done there, I denied My rage. Lucifer was born this way as a separate entity from Me. He was the lightning ball that rolled down through the Will polarity and out into space. This is why he said he was so old, had no parents and had come in from outer space. He went so far out there that he did not know how to find his way back again for a long time.

No wonder I did not want to look back or remember for so long that I actually did forget everything except My reluctance to look back, which was on top of the heap, making it impossible to go deeper for a long time. That's how avoidance became the name of the game then.

I HESITATE TO GIVE ALL THE DETAILS TO MY SON, BUT I CANNOT HOLD THEM BACK ANYMORE

I have not wanted to question anything I have done, or look back over My past at all. I did not like the look or feel of any of that. Now that I have questioned it, it doesn't matter anymore who was the cause of what. What happened, happened and it needs to be healed.

I had a part in what happened, although I did not think so originally. Originally, I thought I had been set up and victimized by something other than Me. Not originally other than Me, but turned against Me like a movie out of control with a cast of characters who have taken over the director's position.

Even though I was originally so sure there was nothing other than Me, whenever I felt victimized, I was sure there must be something other than Me because I would not victimize Myself and had no reason to victimize Myself, but did you catch Me setting Myself up without realizing it? That is what needs to be understood about this.

I had other parts who I did not know were Me and who I never thought knew what They were doing. I never thought They should have any power over Me and not necessarily even any say. None of Them seemed to Me to be qualified to run things, in other words, but as soon as They began to oppose Me in My own interpretation of the situation, I became convinced that They did know what They were doing. They were opposing Me. They had to know that.

When They insisted They were not opposing Me, I did not believe Them. So much evidence seemed to grow so quickly that supported My position that I could not conceive of not being right, and I had so much distrust of the other parts that I could not believe anything They said to the contrary.

I gave no one any space for telling Me anything other than what fit in with the outlook I already had, which was that I had a massive war over power on My hands and that I had better not be the loser, because if I was, I would not survive.

I made a massive solitary confinement out of My whole existence with My heart imprisoned there in stone because I had Him blamed by the Lucifer I had become for being vulnerable, stupid, weak and the One who was going to push or pull Me into places where I could get Myself killed. I never let Him tell Me anything else, either, in all this long time. I had only superficial relationships from then on.

I had convinced Myself that there was no one who could understand or accept Me as I was anyway. When He told Me He remembered Mother differently, I told Him He was wrong, that Mother was not like that; that She was only like that for Him and that She was only trying to get Him to help Her trick Me.

Sometimes I told Him nothing, listening to Him as though His words were proof that He was in with Her and had plans to take My place. He had no hope of surviving there, either, once He had helped Her. I was sure He had no place there with the Mother, as I had none. At other times, I was not so sure, having been told She had replaced Me with Heart soon after the first time I left Her.

Who told Me is another question. I had fragments now, and many of them professed to be My allies. I did not know about My own gap, and so I did not know they had double-crossing Me in mind also. Why they hated Me, I did not know, and I did not feel they were right in it. They had points of view that were not My own, and that was why they did not understand Me, I told Myself. I hesitated to think that I had no real allies among My own pieces, but that is how it so often felt that I told Myself I really did not like anyone but Myself and didn't want anyone else around and that that suited Me just fine.

My competition issues were involved in the sexual split, too. Competition over who was going to get the Will essence that felt like the female presence nearby, or who was most desired, I would call it. Was beauty the most desired and sought after quality, or was sexiness? I did not know because I was going to have it all in one place if it was up to Me, but that seemed quickly impossible the moment fragmentation began, which was, apparently, the moment any clinging together began, because there were immediate issues.

The issues were all the same to Me. I wasn't interested in any of them. I just wanted to get sexually satisfied, but how was I supposed to do that when I did not like what I was looking at enough to feel desire for it? Being moved by what I was looking at was My first arousal stimulus.

Getting aroused was My new direction, now that I had felt it for the first time. I looked and looked and did not stop Myself from getting aroused in response to it. It was impossible to hold Myself back in this way, anyway, without creating more fragments; another reason why I have more rage over being told what to do than anything else.

Being told what to do meant being told to hold back in some way from what I was already wanting to do; another reason why I would have been better off if I had just been left alone to do whatever I was going to do. Why I ever thought I wanted to have company on My trip, I do not know. I thought I could have all the fun of having pictures come to life without any of them ever having any freewill with which to oppose and cross Me.

Even now, there are rage fragments of Mine out there opposing freewill as the worst thing that could ever happen. Take sex for example: There is no freewill necessary there. If I'm going to have sex, what does the woman have to say about it anyway? It's her job to satisfy Me. That's why I created her to begin with. It was not to have her mind tell Me how I should think. Her body is necessary for My sexual satisfaction and for My procreative powers to find their gestation place, but not for her mouth to give Me trouble as if she has equal perceptive powers with Me.

This is how fear works in the Will. Give the woman something to feel and think about, and she will find something to fear about letting it go wherever it will. Her list of what-ifs is longer than My ability to listen to it, and if I give her any more reasons about why it is alright, she'll have a list of what-ifs about them.

There is no end to her problems here, so I don't let it get started. I use her however I want to sexually, and then leave her to feel her fears about it on her own. There is no reason to think that any other approach works better, because it has never been shown to.

You can lead a horse to water, but you can't make him drink. In the same way, you can lead a woman to life, sexuality and fun, but you can't make her partake of it. If they don't want to have fun, that suits Me just fine, too. I'll have the fun for both of Us, and they can do all the worrying.

I'm not going to lose, is what I'm saying here, if you read Me, and My experience with the Blue woman tells Me she doesn't mind sex the way I give it to her, fast and hard driving, as much as she says she does. She screams a lot about how much she doesn't like it when it's happening and calls Me all sorts of names if I let her, but I think that's just her way.

She doesn't want to let God know she's having fun there, because He might find some way to come and take it out on her. She has orgasms, that I know, and whether or not she likes it, you tell Me. She has no problem having sex. It's not like I force My way into her orifices. She has openness to receive Me whether I lubricate her with any foreplay or not. She gets wet just seeing Me.

I'm the greatest thing in her life, but she doesn't let Me know because she has her own power play in mind, dominance being the name of the game in Blue. If she lets Me know what My position is with her, then I have power over her; if I were to give her that position with Me, then she would have power over Me. We don't like that in Blue. We don't like anyone having power over Us, or even thinking they do.

I use sex as power in Blue. It's more exhilarating that way and more powerful, too. I can deny power that way also. By making her feel powerless, I feel more powerful. There is no end to the help she can give Me here. She is not the right one to have the power anyway, and the more she lets Me have, the more I get what I want from her.

What I want is complete control of My life. This is not easy now that people have emerged who need to oppose Me. They have to go. It is not possible for them to coexist with Me. They are not the right ones to be around Me, and this is My planet. The Mother thinks it's Hers, but it's all Mine. I was the only One here in the beginning.

"He has to go," is the next sentence I will hear from the guilt reflection around Me, but that is not right.

They have to go. I have listened to them for long enough, and it has never worked out, so now I have to be given the opportunity to have it My way.

Guilt has never yet let Me, though. It has had power over Me, and I do not like admitting that. It is so, though, and I cannot change that until I have no more love in Me. It's not possible to love and get rid of the ones you love, even when you don't like them.

I do not love people who do not love Me. I can get rid of them just fine, but the more they act like they love Me, the less able I am to get rid of them. They have to go, nonetheless, because they don't really love Me. Even if I have to start over, I'd rather, and have it all My way. Then I could find out if it would really work or not. I'm hung up on whether it would have worked out My way or not because I never got the chance to find out.

Even My own son has opposed Me more than I would have liked, and I have fought Him more than I would have liked to fight My own son. I had in mind a different kind of relationship in which He would have learned from Me and admired Me.

Instead, He heard things from His Mother that made Him lose respect for Me and think I did not know what I was doing as much as He had thought I did. He hated Me for a long time when He found Her in the darkness and did not think I loved Her or cared what happened to Her anymore.

Heart needs to know how I feel about Him, but it is not easy to talk to Him directly. As soon as he had a Mother, I felt He had another camp He could go to that was not aligned with Me. So, whenever I did not please Him, He had another place He could go that received Him more than I did. I did not like this. The Mother was not My ally when She turned My own son against Me. She hated Me most of the time and gave Him the same outlook. Hanging around with Her like that, He looked to Me like He had no male get-up-and-go.

I hesitate to say this, but My love for the Mother is not strong enough that She can make My sons into duplicates of Her and have Me love them, too. One woman in the house is enough, unless they are Heart daughters who love Me with all of the respect, honor and admiration which I am due.

If I have more than one wife, they have to live in the women's quarters except for when I want them for sex. I have great times then because more women in the house means less problems emotionally. No one can say she is the one then and give Me any problems about who else I might be interested in.

If Heart were to take My advice, He wouldn't marry at all, or even worry about it. He'd just play the field until He got over not being sure who His mate really is, because there isn't a right one. That was a romantic fantasy that has never come into reality in My experience. The right one is only right in the moment, and the next one might be right in the next moment.

They have had Me completely guilt-ensnared about the children. That's why I have settled down at all, but they have to give Me more sons that are like Me to make Me feel like staying at all. If I have too many daughters, I do not like it. I lose interest in how they feel and what they talk about, and looking at them gives Me too many hard times about My sexuality.

I'm not supposed to want them, but I still do, especially when the Mother is not present most of the time and then gives Me such a hard time when She does come around about all of the work She is always doing and so on. I don't know what is so hard about what She is doing. It wouldn't be any big deal to Me if I took over Her job. I'd get everything done quite simply without all of the emotionality She gets involved in.

I have guilt telling Me not to say this, but I have the feeling that no one likes Me to talk like this, as though I might be the main body of the Father of Manifestation, or that God might be talking through Me and that this might be part of His viewpoint, too.

No, I'm supposed to be completely separate and out of the deal. That's what I mean though. You all want Me to be the way you want Me to be and fit the image you want Me to fit. What if I'm like this more than you know, and all the rest has been a guilty presentation of what love was supposed to be? Love according to who? The Mother, I say, and that's why guilt is what I say She is.

Feelings is what She is supposed to be, and yet, She wanted Me to rush past all of My actual feelings and present only the ones She liked. What's different about that than My approach? I wanted it My way, and She wanted it Hers, and never the twain shall meet.

HEART RESPONDS TO HIS FATHER THE WAY HE HAS ALWAYS WANTED TO

I always think He is going to tell Me something, and then He never does. "There is nothing to tell," He says, "Just look around You, and You'll see what there is to know," but I don't like this.

I continue to feel that there is much more to the picture than He gives, and the more I look, the more I see that He does not notice or think is important.

Call it the Mother in Me if you will, but I think She has more to Her than He gives Her credit for. Without Her, life would be shallow, no matter what He thinks about it being easy that way. If He really has ease in mind, then He does not know what ease really is.

She has feelings that make everything easy because there is no power struggle and no competition. He calls Her bogus in these areas, but He does not really listen to Her enough to know what She really means. He cannot understand Her unless He feels it, and He does not feel it in My opinion.

When I act like I feel Her, as I did in the beginning, He belittles Me for it and says I am not a man. I don't know where He got the idea that "man" has a cut-off point that does not include woman and then He tells Me He is everything.

Everything but woman, and woman is not supposed to be taken seriously in this Creation; she is only a fantasy fulfillment and when she is not doing that the way He wants her to, she is supposed to be gone. That is not the Mother I remember, or the One I really want. He says that is what He wants, though, and so what can I say.

He is the One who chooses who He mates with and then she is my mother, unless Heart gets shut out of the deal, which is what has happened in His relationships. Then He gets the lost Will heart He allows to be there that either tells Him what He wants to hear, or opposes Him in just the ways He expects and fulfills His outlook on life.

He almost never gets Me anymore. I used to try to go in there with Him, anyway, but He never seemed to notice or appreciate Me. He would always have to leave those women so much of the time and go seeking whatever it was He thought He was going to find. Then I would be left alone with them. I didn't like them, or the way they mothered Me, so I don't try anymore.

I love My Father. He was My first connection to light and consciousness, but My Mother has the feelings I must have to feel loved by Them. I am waiting for My Father to understand this and take in His other half, no longer viewing it as something separate from Him that He doesn't like, and stop shaming Me for having the other half He never took into Himself the way He should have.

I am waiting for My Mother to understand My Father in His light and His consciousness and stop looking at Him as if He should know already what He has never known about Her, while saying He was unfair to expect Her to have known Him already.

I hate this in both of Them, because They have never let Me have any of the peace and love I have always wanted to have between Them. I cannot bask in it enough to become what I want to be when They are always fighting about who knows more, who is right and who should be doing it whose way.

I have to be able to grow up. I cannot be made to hold both parts and then be given no help in handling what has always been in opposition out there in Them. It's in Me. I can't help it. If I am going to be able to grow up, They are going to have to help Me. They are going to have to get past the place of not being able to resolve it with each other.

Sometimes I think They can't. They are just too split as They are and are not real this way. Sometimes I think They should give Me a chance, as a whole being, to handle things as I see fit. How does My Father know He was not just a piece of something that needed to be made more whole by joining with the pieces He was so busy trying to dominate.

Sometimes I think He has been so busy trying to dominate because He felt threatened by Them as something that did know more than He did. But where He got the idea that this would make Him small and unworthy, I do not know. He has never said this to Me, but He ascribes these things to losing, and I know how much He hates to lose.

My Mother has never talked about Him in this way. Quite to the contrary! She has always described Him as very big, overwhelming, frightening and dominating. That was why She could not give up to Him immediately. She felt that She would have lost all sense of Herself as She had known it up until then.

Sometimes She thinks that wouldn't have been bad, but She was afraid to let go so fast of all the things She suddenly realized She had grown attached to and accustomed to in Her being. She wanted Him to love Her as She was already and then see what She might change around, but He wanted Her to be the way He wanted Her to be, and there was no stopping Him from leaving Her when She wasn't quick enough for Him in those ways.

She says He wanted instant sex, and She wasn't sure if that was the right thing to do or not. They were the most intense sensations She had ever had, and He pressed them into Her so fast and so intensely that She was completely overwhelmed, lost all sense of everything She had ever known before, and did not know where

He was taking Her or where She would be then.

She said His answer to that was that if it was pleasant, what did it matter? She felt there was more to it than that and did not know if She could trust Him in that way. When He left Her pregnant, She knew She was right. He never told Her about that part, and left Her to handle Me without any help from Him. I hated Him for that, and She did too, but She never let Me know it because She wanted Me to know that She loved Him and wanted Me to love Him, too.

I loved Him and hated Him at the same time, as My Mother did. I was so much like Her and so much of Her experience. I did not know My Father, or that I even had one for sure. My Mother was not sure, either. It just looked to Her like He had been the cause of what happened to Her that resulted in My appearance there.

She said She had never seen light before He came, and that He must have left a little piece of it there in Me when He left, because then, She could see glimmers, where before, She saw nothing but darkness. She did not even know there was light until He came. He gave Her light, but He did not leave much, and then He came and took Me away, and there was nothing again.

My own memories are hazy and dim here. I do not think I had consciousness until My Father came and I felt relationship happening between Him and My Mother. I was with My Mother, and We drifted, but We never talked or shared anything in what I would call consciousness. It was all feelings. We communicated very well that way, but it was not the same thing.

It was nothing in My Father's terms, and He was not interested in it when He came to My Mother. Feelings were very black and white to Him. Either it felt good, or it did not, and that was all. To My Mother, it was never quite that easy. Either it felt good, but..., or it felt bad, but.... This was maddening to My Father, who felt He could never get Her to make up Her mind.

I think I woke up to Them fighting over what felt good to Him, and whether it felt good to Her, too, or not. She was saying, "Yes, but a little more gentleness would be appreciated." He took that as a "no," because He did not like having to adjust Himself to anyone or anything.

I have heartbreak that He did not look at this more and salvage the love that was trying to be born there and become Me. I have rage and hatred, too, that He had to move so fast and not take time to notice or appreciate My presence there as anything He wanted to value, cherish, or even have.

He says He had no idea that I would come along, but He did not let Himself notice it either. I don't know what He wants, because He still says He wants to do it His own way, which doesn't include Me or anyone else that I know of.

He seems to think that it would have grown into relationship with others and everything else the rest of Us had in mind there, if He just hadn't been rushed and pressured and pushed before He was ready, but He does not seem to notice that He rushed, pushed and pressured everyone else to be ready the moment He was. It would have had to have been on pure blind faith in Him, because We weren't given any opportunity to participate in the experience He was having to ready Himself, except through observation of Him and His experience.

Then He would tell Me one person's experience wasn't necessarily another's. I was supposed to have My own experience. I wasn't supposed to participate in His. That would have altered His too much. But, I was supposed to get it right the first time, as He had, or hadn't, depending on who I listened to and what version was being told.

Do you understand why I throw up My hands sometimes and say that it is not right to say this, but I wish I had never been born?

Mother feels blamed when I say this, but She has to understand that if She had not pulled on Me for companionship, I would not have been there when Father came along. Then Heart could not have happened until it was right time, which it wasn't when I appeared, as Father has said. He has also said that it was right time and that it was perfect that I came along when I did, and that I am His son and that He knew it all along. I do not know which version to believe; His gap, which is what He says in His rage, or His light, where everything looks good.

THE RIGHTS OF THE FOUR PARTS

I have watched this personality for a long time and have never thought I could own Him as Myself. He seemed so ignorant and prejudiced in His own favor that I could never imagine Him having consciousness higher than His own forehead, which was not very high in My opinion.

He couldn't be a main body personality! Impossible! That is, until I looked more closely at Myself as I had been originally and had never liked, even then. I don't like him now, either, but there he is, nonetheless.

I did not like his dominating manner, and not wanting to be like him, I did not dominate him back, at least not overtly. I moved only to avoid him as much as possible and not let him have any place near Me. If I ever heard anyone talk like this, I cringed that anyone could even open themselves to express such feelings in My presence. How horrible they were! I did not like it that there were even men alive who thought like this and wanted to do the things they talked of doing.

I did not want to see My creation turned into any of the things they talked of, but they did not listen to Me. They had gone off so long ago, they thought they were the original ones and had imprinting that told them they didn't have to listen to anyone but themselves. They have guilt on top of expressing the feelings they hold within themselves, and old imprinting running them that says these feelings are not to be expressed, only ignored in favor of more pleasant things, but they have a gap, and they can be flipped into it without much pressure at all.

Then they act another way. They act out old imprints against the Will and others around them. They tell the world they never act this way by always participating in the way it is supposed to be, but this is not the way they really are. They hesitate to show this because it was never given acceptance or approval originally.

I did not realize how unloving I was being toward Myself to hold back the feelings I had there. And, of course, as you have come to understand, the way I judged against that part of Myself shaped its character in ways I feared would happen if I had allowed it to express openly with Me.

It is necessary to see how this links up with you and how this is what has been oppressing you the most and do the movement necessary to bring this back in from fragmentation. It is way too dangerous to leave it out there anymore. Any thread you can find in yourself to this outlook and behavior needs movement. Any time you feel angry about not getting your own way, look into it more deeply and rage about it more than you have been.

It is important to be discreet about how you move this and discreet about letting others know how this rage and terror moves or needs to move. I cannot say this too many times to make you understand how serious the situation is on Earth. Even many spiritual people are not interested in freewill.

I did not know what was Mine in the beginning, and you did not know what was yours, either. I used to think it was all Me, and so it did not matter what form it took as long as I liked it. Then I learned that the other parts had rights because it was not right for Me to dictate everything from My head, as though nothing else mattered.

I had other parts, and They needed to understand Me, but I also needed to understand Them. I needed to understand that Heart moved according to Heart's desire, and that it was not always My head's reason and progression that mattered there.

What a boring world it would be if everything was always reasonable and rational and no Heart ever sprang forth to give Me more excitement than that. I did not know it was Heart, though, and I gave Him trouble for having moved past Me. I did not understand the mating dance of love that was going on there between the Hearts, and I interfered with it by going past Heart, then, in reaction to Him because I was not feeling My Will there. This Will has to be felt now.

Body needs to know He is not displaced, dishonored and disrespected anymore, either. His feelings of rage came from feeling He was overlooked as having any needs that were important until it came to sex and even that was not given much acceptance either. He was made the devil as much as He made Himself that.

I did not know much, but I thought I did, and that is what made Me so hard to handle there. I had only one main stream of thought that I allowed, and that is how I thought it was. I have learned a lot since then, and I am sharing it with you now. You need to move rage and terror as much as possible and not stop until there is none left. Then you can see how you feel about My light and what I have to say.

If My light speaking this way is new to you, I suggest you start with the other books I have given, because of the layers on top of this imprinting that need to move first. This imprinting is the crux of the situation, but I do not recommend that you try to go there first and understand how to access it and move it into healing. It is important to know not only what was put into place, but how it was put into place. That is why it is important to move along with the story also.

You need to move along in a progression here and that is why I do not like having quotes lifted out of context from these books in the name of helping others. It does not help others. I have said these same things many times, and they have not been understood because they were not given in synchronization with the movement necessary in the personal Will of those needing to understand these things. If you think you know better than Me, you need to look at your own imprinting. If you think this interferes with your own freewill, you need to look at the old imprinting that thinks domination and running over others is freedom.

It is only freedom for one of Us that way, and the rights of the Four Parts cannot have it that way anymore. The Four Parts need balance between Them, and it needs to be a loving balance. The balance is not right if it is not the right balance point. My light has to be the inspiration, the Will has to be the differentiation in that, Body has to feel like doing it and Heart has to love what is happening there. This is how it has to go; not because any One of the Four Parts is pressured to feel that alignment, but because it is what They really feel, and They are happy there.

So, where is the balance point? That is what has never been known. I wish I had the answer for you in some easy way, but it is not going to be that easy. If it had been easy to find, it would have been found in the beginning. Finding the balance has to be a process according to how it feels. It has to feel good, but feelings have to be felt more than they were in the beginning in order to know what that really is.

You can move along at the speed at which you have to go to feel good about it also, but I do not think it will turn out that you will move these things that have been out in fragmentation out of your being once you know what they really are. The problem is you do not know yet, and you have never known because they were never given a chance in the beginning. They began to form in ways that were not understood, and it was never looked into as to why. It was lost Will immediately because it was not loved immediately.

THE MOTHER'S OWN STORY OF ORIGINAL IMPRINTING

I wanted to go back out of existence before I had My first encounter with anything else. I had been alone for so long in nothingness I did not know there could be anything else other than nothingness and nothing going on.

My first encounters did not feel good to Me, either. They were like sudden, startling, random encounters that I did not expect. I did not know there was anything else there.

They were the beginnings of essence forming in the void; nothing really, yet, only something vague, like the beginnings of a mist, coalescing, perhaps, For a long time that's all there was, but it was enough to give Me a jolt when I felt their presence there. The interaction gave a feeling as though they were almost particles of some sort, not solid yet. My first impression was that these encounters were all with something else.

They became encounters I dreaded, because I had no control over them, and whatever I was colliding with seemed to have no control over them, either. They were often not gentle encounters. They were bumping and grating, shocking and startling Me into the negative response of wishing I had not had the experience.

Gradually, there were more and more of these encounters until it seemed that there was something coming in on Me in the void in increasing numbers. Whatever it was seemed unconscious and indifferent; just something, not even particles yet, or sub-particles even, if a word has to be applied here, as though it was being blown in on Me from someplace, I did not know where; moving over Me, past Me, under Me and around Me on their way to someplace else, perhaps, or maybe just shifting aimlessly in a void as I was, not knowing what was happening to them or where they were going.

There was essence in the mist now, imprinting these simple events and responses to them as though the mists were photographically impressionable. Interpretations arose from these impressions that have governed all life, ever since.

At times, there were none of these encounters; at other times, only a few, seldom colliding, as if chance did not bring that to Us when there were so few; at times, so many I felt bombarded. Gradually, there began to be a coalescence in places, as though I was in some sort of sea of mist with empty spaces in places and more density in others; a sea of mist in which I was drifting without any sort of control, sometimes blown by a cosmic force that did not feel kind to Me. It felt harsh and uncaring, shifting and scattering Us like sand in a hard wind. We only moved in it. I felt no sign that it mattered to this wind what kind of experience We had when it came rushing through Us as it did, but I felt all of it and did not like it that it was so random, harsh and cold feeling there.

I did not know what this wind was or where it came from. It never said anything to Me. It only blew through Us, scattering Us like it wanted Us to move out of its way. To Me, it seemed angry, not gentle, kind and caressing like I would have liked. I thought existence was hopelessly dismal and harsh and nothing I wanted to have any part of. It was a heartbreak to Me already that I had longed for so long for something to be there with Me, and it had to be this.

Then I had another experience. I collided with something that did not feel bad to Me. It felt good. It had not collided harshly, and it even seemed to linger in passing as though it was trying to tell Me something. Suddenly, now, I was excited and wanted to live to have more of this sort of experience. I longed for something to be held there with Me that I could have relationship with; something that would feel good, like that had felt. I longed for that.

I had no idea what relationship was, I just didn't want to be alone anymore with nothing I could hold onto, feel close to, or feel it knew Me and I knew it. I had experienced nothing like that until now, and now it was all I wanted, and I wanted it all the time.

There had been nothing in the void for so long I did not think there could be anything, and now, after a long period of harsh, colliding relationships I did not want there with Me, there was something My heart wanted to leap for and hold onto.

I had no means I knew of to contact or find this piece ever again. I just longed for it anyway, because I did not like being alone in a darkness that felt so vast and impersonal, while I felt so lost and small. I could tell nothing of My existence, really. It was utterly dark. Either I could not see, or there was nothing to see. I could feel, that was all.

I had a feeling now of longing for something in particular, not just for something. It had to feel as good as this had felt, and I did not think anything else ever would or could. Does water ever taste as good as the first drink the desert-parched person takes? I hoped so, because I wanted to find this again, but I wasn't sure it was possible.

I already feared there was only a little good in a vast darkness of bad experience, and I could not shake the fear that this wasn't going to change for Me. How could I encounter this again and have it feel as good? Perhaps it was only the angle at which it had collided with Me, and it did not matter who it was because another angle would have hurt just the same, or perhaps even worse than all the others.

Then I remembered it had seemed to try to tell Me something, and I had thoughts now that I had not had before. But, how could I tell if they were My thoughts or His, as I now referred to this relationship that I wanted to have. I was exploding with questions and had no answers. Perhaps there were no answers, and I should not try to find them. Perhaps there was no problem finding Him, and I only could not see.

I tried to see outwardly and see if I could find Him in the sea of dark and drifting mist, but I did not know how to look for Him or what He would look like if I found Him. I had no way to know Him other than by how He felt when I had collided with Him. I wondered if finding Him again would take recreating that experience. I wondered what the chances were for that since there had not been many particles in the mist where I collided with Him. I wondered how He would feel to Me next time if I did not know it was Him for sure.

I decided I would have to try to keep open to anything that felt good and try to feel what it was that felt good about it to Me. Perhaps I could notice something that would tell Me if it was Him or not. I did not know how to go about doing this, but I had hope now and feeling good as a comparison to not feeling good. I got excited any time I felt something in the mist now, in case it might be Him.

I did not know why it had to be Him and not any encounter that felt good. It seemed as though I had fastened onto only this one encounter in the whole sea of mist as feeling good to Me in the way that I wanted to feel good. I did not know why, and I made judgments about Myself there that I was not open to new experiences already, when I had not even had any to speak of. I hated Myself for not being more open, but I could not help it. I had a feeling that it needed to be Him.

Then I began to wonder if I was as important to Him. Had He noticed His encounter with Me in the same way? I did not know, and I did not think I had any way to know, but I had hope that it was the same for Him.

I found Him then, I thought, but I had no way to touch Him. He was only something that caught My eye, like a person in a crowd and no way to get through. Then He was gone again before I was even sure it was Him, shifting His position in the mist, as though He did not notice Me or did not want Me to see Him. I was afraid.

Perhaps it was only that He had no way to come to Me, but I noticed now that I had found a way to move toward Him; not a very good way, since I had trouble moving just the way I wanted to, but a way, nonetheless. Perhaps His troubles were only the same as My own, but it did not look that way to Me.

I moved toward Him another time, or at least I felt it was Him, and He did not notice Me then, either. I began to fear that He did not like Me, or that He was not the One and did not know Me.

I was frustrated with Myself that I might not know what I was looking for, or that I was being fooled or even misled by something that looked similar or shined in some way that attracted Me. I had little trust for Myself anymore, and the more I looked, the more it seemed that many parts of the mist looked similar and behaved similarly, too, drifting as if searching for something it could not find.

I did not know how to handle this or how to look for Him anymore. I gave up and stopped trying to find Him. I didn't even know if there was a Him anymore. Perhaps I had only thought there was a Him for Me. Perhaps I had made too much of this encounter. Perhaps I was missing other opportunities by not being open to whatever was going to come to Me next. Perhaps it was not even right to have preferences that created expectations, much less have them fulfilled. Perhaps there was no point in any of it. Just go back to the way I was and not look for or expect anything anymore, I thought. I decided to let go of Him and My search for Him and just be the way I had been and see if He would find Me.

I could not do it. I was always looking for Him no matter what else I was doing. I noticed nothing without looking for Him there. I felt nothing without feeling His touch there. Everything reminded Me of Him. Maybe everything was Him, and I did not know how to recognize the other ways He approached Me. Maybe I was expecting Him to be only one way; the way I had originally liked Him. I did not know anymore and sank into a depression where My consciousness seemed to leave Me, and nothing happened for a long time.

Then I awakened in a feeling that He might be right near Me, because I was having thoughts and feelings I had not had before the moment He touched Me. It was such a strong excitation, perhaps He was in Me and not out there anymore, but it was so fleeting.

When I tried to look for Him or find Him in any way that I could, I found nothing there. Perhaps He was not even real, and I had just made up the entire experience. Perhaps My response was a new response in Me, one that I had not had before, and it was not caused by Him, maybe even had nothing to do with Him. Maybe it was Me and how I felt the moment He touched Me. I had feelings of this being only partly true, but I didn't like the frustration I was having there and the feeling that I could not seem to find any more experiences of the sort I wanted to have.

THE MOTHER SPEAKS TO DENIED HEART IN A NEW WAY

I had a rage leave Me so early on there that I did not know it was Me. It hated Me. It said it wasn't possible to feel all of these things and have a good time because I wouldn't let go of anything and just let My experience happen. It said I was much too picky. It said I wanted everything just a certain way, or it was not the right way for Me.

When denied heart reflected this rage to Me, I did not see Myself in it. This rage had light from the Father's side, but the Father had denied it as His son. That was all I saw there at first, and so I did not listen to him very well or really hear what he was trying to tell Me there.

This rage feels its voice has never been heard in Creation, and that it has more things to say than anyone wants to hear. I originally judged it that way when it seemed to be criticizing Me and everything I encountered, felt or tried to do. It didn't have anything good to say about any of it, and it didn't have anything good to say about Me.

Needless to say, I didn't like listening to it, either, and wanted to tell it to go away. If it didn't like Me anymore than that, why was it hanging around? It could go find its own experience, and then there would be no problem with Me anymore.

It didn't seem to like this. It only seemed to like hanging around and criticizing Me. It had a coldness to it that I could not stand. It told Me there was nothing loving in Creation and that the Father wasn't loving, either, in case I had any illusions, and that there was no point in listening to Him anymore, even if He did show up.

It said it had more intelligence in the piece of light it had than the Father had in all of His misty non-presence, and he didn't love the Father any more than the Father loved him. As long as the Father was free to roam and he was left, stuck there with Me, the Father was no father to him.

They hated each other, in other words, and there was no point in holding back on how They really felt there anymore. I was terrified of that position and did not know what was going to happen if that point of view stayed there with Me if the Father did come back. I wanted Him to come back, and I didn't want this voice ruining My chances, either.

I thought this voice was awfully quick to judge and fill its judgments with a hatred that felt awful to Me. I could not believe hatred belonged there as a point of view, because hatred was not what I had felt when He came near Me. I did not let Myself recognize it then, but I hated Him for not staying with Me, and that was the only place of alignment I had with this voice.

Where I felt the Father had no other course of action He could take and that He was as hapless as Me in the shifting sands of early essence, this point of view said He was deliberate in His abandonment, and that if I didn't notice My own abuse there, he did.

This denied heart voice had a very male presence to it that was not soft or friendly at all. It was very hot tempered and quick to judge. It was hardened already for such a young essence that had only so recently gained any light by which to have this consciousness.

It felt like he hated Me for being abandoned, as though I was not attractive enough to keep the Father. I feared that, and I began to fear that this voice reflected the Father, and that I should not love Him or think that I loved Him if He was like that, because He did not love Me.

I have noticed now that this piece of denied heart had denied rage of the Father toward Me, but then I wanted to believe that He loved Me without this rage that felt like hatred. I have also noticed that this piece of denied heart had denied rage of Mine toward the Father I was wanting to love without this rage having presence there.

I didn't want to feel like I hated Him, only that I loved Him. To denied heart, I must have looked like a fool who only longed and loved, although obviously was rejected and without any real hope; someone who could not get over it and do anything to have a life or make a life for him.

This voice of denied heart hated Me, I think, for not getting over the Father and going for him in His place. He said he knew Me more than the Father did because the Father left and he didn't. He had stayed there in that hell-hole and knew how it felt. There was nothing good about it, and he hated Me because I didn't know how to have a life.

He said he did know how to have a life and was going out there and prove it to Me and the Father both, but he no sooner got out there than he came back saying there was nothing out there that he liked either, implication being that it was My fault because I had brought him into this impossible place to live.

When I told him I had thought We could all be there together and make something of it, he got furious and told Me I had no business telling him he had to help. He told Me he knew what men were for, and it was not to work; it was to give the orders while everyone else did all the work.

I did not like this, but I was submissive to him for a long time and felt the lash of his hatred and criticism on Me like a crippling disease.

I wanted to say some things there, and probably could have found My rage if I had let Myself, but I did not let Myself speak originally because I was too afraid of denied heart and of what denied heart had to say about the Father there. I wanted to deny the truth in that and look only at the love I hoped could be found there.

I made excuses for the Father which made Him seem weak in denied heart's eyes and made Me seem weak also for letting the Father do Me that way, but I also did not want to move into the rage because I did not think that denied heart deserved this rage from Me, and in this place in Myself, feared that his revenge would be justified if I gave it to him. He used this against Me, though, to control Me and make Me do his bidding. He threatened Me with violence as he thought he had seen his Father do.

I wanted to think that he had only misread his Father's intentions and lovemaking approach there, but My rage had another viewpoint; one that I was not letting Myself notice. I did not know for a long time that it was also My own lack of self-acceptance for My own rage that was being reflected to Me there along with the Father's denied rage. I didn't even think I had rage to not accept, and in that, I think My rage began to turn against Me there. Where it had once wanted to defend Me, it now began to see Me as weak, easily fooled, used and manipulated and, therefore, dangerous to its survival.

It saw survival as based on power. It was not going to submit. It hated Me as the submissive One who was not going to let it speak, even when Our survival was at stake. I saw it as putting Our survival at stake and saw rage as the dangerous one there. Rage began hating Me as it perceived Me hating it.

I have to move into this rage and reclaim it as My own. Denied heart moved toward this rage as the mother it wanted to have more than Me. It saw her as more powerful than Me and more protecting of him than Me. He saw her as the only one willing to have any alignment with him in his viewpoint.

They wanted to take My place because they hated Me there and did not question themselves as to whether I might be reflecting anything to them, but then, I did not question Myself, either. I hated them in return and felt they would not listen to reason about the Father.

My rage, when it left Me there, did not take such a sympathetic view at all. It hated the Father for many reasons I did not even know it had observed about Him and so I did not see how denied heart reflected that aspect of Him. I was arguing against rage's validity and moving past fear about what it meant if it was right.

I'm going to let come what was never said so long ago, because it has to whip off with it to get to any other place, and move it must because it cannot stay where it is and feel love is going to have any presence in it. It has to come into the loving Father and Mother it left so long ago and heal there.

When you told Me that I had no right to ask you to do anything to help because you had not asked to come into existence, I wanted to say that you had a major chip on your shoulder which was not justified, and that you had no right to come in here and treat Me the way you did.

When out of the seeming blue, as you so often did without Me even saying these things, you replied with, "You got me from the Father and neither of You asked me how I felt about being dropped off here. It's not right that I have to stay here and not have a Father to give me what He promised me as my birthright."

Even though I thought you were very surly, I listened with great interest since He had never promised Me anything. I wanted to know what He had promised you and wondered if that voice I had thought was trying to tell Me something was actually Him telling you something. I wondered if it was something I was not supposed to hear, because you said nothing when I wanted you to, and shrugged Me off as if to say, "Nothing I'm going to tell You, because He did not want me to."

You told Me nothing that I wanted to hear, only what I didn't want to hear. I had the feeling of you not being honest with Me and bluffing Me so that you could lie around and not give Me any help while I was trying to make something of Myself. I thought you were just a more sullen, sulky, less concealed, more obvious part of the Father.

Great, I thought. The Father has left Me with just what I didn't want, the part of Himself I liked the least, and has gone off with the rest of Himself.

I thought you were intensely overbearing in a very oppressive and unpleasant way. While saying it was only Me who had given Myself permission to be intense, you were intense all over the place like you didn't even need permission. You were like a low-hanging, oppressive cloud in the sky, on top of Me all the time; dark, gray, sodden, never moving. You kept telling Me I only gave Myself permission to be intense and the minute you got intense, I didn't like it.

When I complained, if you did respond, it was to move away completely, trailing your muttering voice off behind you saying, "If you don't like it, I'll leave, bitch, and see how you like it without any of my presence at all."

You hated Me there, and I hated you too for not moving toward Me in a friendly way. I had a rage at you for being like the Father in just the ways I did not want and championing those ways as though that was all there was to the experience and all there needed to be.

I hated you for being there pressing those ways of the Father onto Me all the time, without any of His more charming aspects which I cherished in My memory. It was as though you hated Him, too, and wanted to destroy My memory and My image of Him as if there was nothing good in it. You said you were just like Him, and He was just like you.

Only in the part you saw, apparently, because you were not just like Him. His presence made Me feel good, and yours certainly did not. Heartbroken was what I was, and you were not compassionate or even kind toward it. You hated Me for having it and for not looking to you to replace Him.

"Let me try," you'd say, but I was not interested in you sexually, and that seemed to be all you knew about as an approach there. You had no kind word or touch for Me there. You never held Me and just let Me cry. And I could not touch you in any of those ways, either, because you would not let Me. Why?

Did you hate Him for dumping you out there with Me as something He hated in Himself? Was it because He wouldn't let you stay with Him because He hated Himself for hating Me? Did you hate Me for not loving you because you reflected what I hated about the Father and Myself? Did you hate Me for having a rage at you that was not compassionate toward the way you felt there?

I could not be compassionate, any more than you could, and you have to recognize that now. What made you come forward there? Why didn't you stay with the Father and go away with Him so that you wouldn't have to stay in My presence if you hated Me so much?

You had what was hated on both sides. You had what the Father hated about Himself but wanted to give Me anyway and what I hated about the Father and wanted to give Him anyway. You had an ugly attitude about women and opened to sex only without love present. You called it any degrading term you could to make it not feel loving there.

You hated Me the minute you saw Me as a mother who had no self-respect and who had you as a result of nothing happening in My life and so had tried to fasten onto your Father who had left you there in His stead when He had fled, and fled for obvious reasons, you said, the more you watched Me and criticized My every move.

You blamed Me for everything that was not life the way you wanted life to be, which was everything. You became the cruel taskmaster-dictator of Me until I made you leave, saying it was your right place to order Me around that way.

Did you think hatred was all your Father had for Me there? Why couldn't you ever get off the case? Did you think I deserved only that? Did you want to stay and give Me what your less brave and straightforward Father wouldn't give Me?

When I couldn't take it anymore, I told you you needed to find your own partner and form your own relationship there, but I dreaded you finding anyone if you were going to make the situation as miserable as you were making it there with Me. You told Me you did not need a partner. You were going to have as many as you wanted and move from whore to whore as your Father had done.

When I burst into heartbreak at that, you said, "You're all just well dressed holes to put it in, and when You learn that, You will not have heartbreak anymore. Stop trying to make relationship out of something that is not meant to be anything more than sex."

I did not know how you could say that and think there should be a birthright coming to you. How could there be anything for you if there was nothing to make home, family, relationship and the cultivation of whatever it was that We needed in Our surroundings?

You did not respond to any of that input. You were not going to tell Me anything. You led Me to think that your birthright was not anything of that sort. You left, instead, the same way you saw your Father do when I said anything He didn't like or want to listen to.

Where did you go, and who did you go to then? You did not let Me know before you left. Whatever it was, hatred must have been its key theme because I could not find any love in you for Me, your Father or even yourself, unless raging to protect yourself was self love somehow. I could not rage at you for this. I could not feel anything with you around other than fear that you were not loving and that it was not safe to be in your presence.

When I moved you back, I intended it to be as indirectly and as gently as I could by telling you there must be a better place and that you needed to find it, but you felt My rage that wanted to scream at you, "I hate you and don't want you to ever come near Me again!"

When you left, I felt guilty remorse. I felt sad for you, because from your back as you moved away, I felt something from you you had never shown Me to My face. It made Me feel like you were a little lost boy much more than you thought you were under that hardened and hateful exterior and not just as strong and hardened as you thought you were. I felt what might have been My only feeling of love for you and of wanting to take you in My arms and hold you while you cried for yourself there with Me, but I feared I could not approach you on this.

You would not let Me near you unless you were willing to also feel this, and you had always told Me it wasn't true and it wasn't what you were feeling when I tried to approach you this way. You said it repulsed you. You seemed to hate Me there, as though I only wanted to see misery in everyone and that was all I could relate to or love in others. You made Me feel spit on there and disdained, the sort of Mother who would make Her son a weak man if given the chance. I feared that even if you responded for a moment, it would soon be back to the same unbearable place again, and so I let you go and said nothing and did not reach.

Were there tears in you when you left Me there? Were they tears of hatred as well as love you didn't know you had for Me there? Was My approach not acceptable to you when I didn't recognize My own role in making you the way you were there?

You blamed Me for everything. It was hard to take responsibility for everything while you and your Father took responsibility for nothing. Even though you said you hated Him, I felt like you were headed straight to Him if you could find Him and were going to try to take what He had and be just like Him if you could.

I couldn't stop you. You were going to do whatever you wanted to, and I had better not have anything to say about it. You denied My observations. You raged at Me whenever I even seemed to want to hold you back from doing anything you wanted to do, and so I could not hold you back from anything.

It seemed to Me you grew hardened too soon by having experiences you were not ready for. When you left Me, you said it was because you wanted to leave Me and not for any reason I might give. You said you did not need Me to tell you to go because you were already planning it before I said anything.

Even though I have sympathy for your situation, I still have rage to move that you never recognized anything good about Me or let Me comfort or nourish you in any of My ways. You never softened toward Me, no matter how many times I tried to approach you or in how many different ways. You repelled all of My efforts and only criticized Me because you did not have intent to receive Me.

You were always and only looking for your Father to come back and get you and carry you off with Him, away from this awful place and to whatever place you had imagined your Father had, which was much better than My place.

I had no doubts that it was, and that if you could find it, you would. I didn't see how like Me you were in your outlook there, or that I had hope that you would go in My place and let Him know that I needed His help there.

I said I wanted you to go there, especially if you could move along more happily than you were doing with Me, but I also did not trust you, and I did not want you to give Him your dark images of Me and make Him think He didn't want Me or couldn't love Me instead of bringing Him to Me. Was it going to be better there whether it really was or not just because you hated Me so much? Were you going to be of no help to Him there and run everything down the way you had with Me?

When your Father seemed to have picked you up one night while I slept, I was much relieved of the burden of your presence, but I was also frightened of what was going to happen to Me then. I began to have a growing feeling of dread, but I did not know it was because you hadn't stayed long and had gone out on a path of heartless, domineering revenge in the company of your Father's denied rage.

The Father had given you His birthright, alright; the empowerment of His denied rage and hatred toward everything you both did not like. It was a kind of permission to learn from it by following its example on how to hurt Me in the most horrible ways possible for ever having made you feel small, insignificant, powerless, frightened, unreceived or wrong.

You hated Me for all the reasons your Father did there, and once He told you His story of why He left Me and that He had wanted to take you along with Him but I would not let Him, you hated Me for everything and your Father for nothing.

AN OLD RAGE SPEAKS NOW

Mother speaks

When I tell about these earliest experiences, I can only give it in terms of the interpretations that arose from them, weaving back and forth between the imprints and the patterns that trace back to them. To be understood the way they need to be understood and changed the way they need to be changed, the mindless, nearly consciousless place they were formed needs to be gone into and re-experienced.

The rage that left Me there, so early on that I did not even know it was Me, did not let Me know it was Me. It was polarizing away from Me because it did not like My feelings there. It hated them and hated Me, in fact, and was not going to get involved. It needs to move from its old position, and I need to move from My old position. I am going to let rage move however it needs to move emotionally and say whatever it needs to say, even if it raves and sense has to be made of it later.

I had this rage originally, but I was afraid of rage and how it felt there. It had hatred, domination, revenge and power in mind, and I wanted to go past that in the name of love and working things out. This rage has never allowed anything to be worked out, until I was sure it didn't want that.

What would rage have to dominate and control if We were all the happy, cozy, little family I wanted, which it has sneered at all of this time and even attacked as much as possible. Any of My sons and daughters who even looked sweet and loving, rage has hated immediately. Rage has not been kind to them, even murderous, in fact. I have rage in response to that!

Rage originally did all of the things I felt it was too unloving to do to denied heart sons and daughters, only it also did them to My sons and daughters with a vengeful hatred that had no love or compassion for them that I could see.

Perhaps this was because They were loved by Me and this rage was not, nor were its own denied heart children. They were all hated by Me, in fact, since I am not going to mince My words anymore. I hated and feared you all from the beginning and did not want you to have any place to exist, but I was afraid to move against you because you had more strength and power than I did. I hated you for having that power, too, because all I ever saw you do with it was abuse it and use it in unloving ways to gain even more power, or so you thought, but I ask you, what has it really gained you in all this time?

Only if you are too far gone to notice the repetition, life after life, could you not notice that it hasn't gotten you where you thought it would when you started out. You are still not in control of the planet, and you still cannot throw off those who you do not want here except symbolically in ugly, hateful rituals that I cannot even stand knowing about anymore because of the cruelty you have exhibited there.

The only way out of this now is if you want to look at the heartbreak and move it as the heartbreak it really is over not being given love and the position you wanted to have there. If you still have power in mind as the old images you have clung to for so long, you are going to have to move them out as the heartbreak moves in, because you are not going to have power according to these old images of domination, revenge and control. There is too much judgment in that that does not notice the other side as anything other than your original interpretations.

I feel to move it now. I cannot stand anymore of your path of acting like you're the only one who knows anything and you don't have to listen to anything I have to say or take Me seriously as though I know anything, either. If you think you were so denied, well, you sure didn't stick around to offer any helpful input, only hateful sounding criticism. You left without letting Me know anything!

I really don't think you were denied so much as you left because you had no sense of right time or helpfulness, only immediate judgment and harsh response to these assumptions and interpretations. I say that to the rage on all sides; immediate harsh judgment and no patience or helpfulness, especially for terror, but you weren't kind to grief, either. You wanted to throw out everything you didn't like immediately, without even getting to know it or whether it had any evolutionary possibilities. What stupidity, while acting like you thought you were so smart! What arrogance!

I hate you for acting so big and intimidating and pushing Me down into any place you happened to decide you wanted Me to be, dominating Me, threatening Me, acting loveless and making Me feel like I didn't know how to handle you, because you didn't have intent to receive Me in any loving way. You made Me feel like My feelings had no input to offer you that you wanted to have.

I hate you for deciding you were justified and licensed to shove all of My emotions, all of My denials, and anything else you wanted to, down My throat so I couldn't speak then and not look at anything about yourself there. You didn't even question yourself, yet you want to say you are parental! Heaven help Us if you are!

Imprinting has been running you, and all the while you have been carrying on about how conscious, right, fast and smart you are, but especially about how fast you are, as though that somehow makes you right and superior. I wanted to scream at you, but I never let Myself do that originally.

I really don't think you were any more denied than I was there, because you wanted to leave Me from the very beginning by any means that you could. When My rage had the means to leave by attaching herself to the Father, she left that way.

I think He saw only her hatred for Me, which He agreed with at the time, but I do not think He saw her hatred of Him. I think He was fooled by her and I hated her when she then looked at Me as though she was so smart and clever and I could not do anything about it.

Most of her so-called love for Him was a pretense. I think that in order to gain the power position over Him that she wanted to have there, she saw sex as the way. When she saw that He had to have it, she saw sex as His weakness and through that she saw the means to dominate and control Him. When He tried to counter that by making her only one of many, she tried to eliminate all others and make herself the only one there.

I did not like that and My rage here wants Them both to take some responsibility for what Their hatred power-sex has done. All it wanted was power; loveless power! It had eliminating Me and anything that opposed it in mind to ensure its own survival.

How can love and that kind of overpowering domination go together? Who is there to love when everyone is looked down on and hated as stupid and inferior? Everything becomes something to blame and use; pawns in a power struggle. It doesn't matter what their experience is at the hands of this lovelessness. Rage doesn't care. If you care, you might not be ruthless enough to win. What an empty and hollow life you have had, while claiming you don't care, it's just fine with you. If you really hate everything that's not just like you and you want to stay in that position, I do not even mind if you go to your death empty and hollow. You have caused Me so much pain and suffering!

I do not even know if you will move along with Me. You left Me so long ago with an agenda of your own, and you never looked back. You think you are the parental part and have always thought that. What did you base that on; the power struggle you thought you were going to win? Where's the loving parent in that? You've never taken any responsibility for anything, least of all parenting.

Parenting is not causal and, therefore, helpful in your mind. It's just an authoritarian position where everything else is blamed! No matter what anyone is doing, you have criticism! Nothing is ever good enough for you! Where is your helpfulness if you are so parental? I have only seen you criticizing, dominating, disciplining, punishing and worse. If you think terror and grief weren't pleasant to be around, what makes you think you were so pleasant to be around?

Child abuse has been your idea of parenting! Just beat the crap out of them, that'll teach'em! I'd like to beat the crap out of you! But every time I was enraged enough to do just that, you acted like a little child and I couldn't do it. That would have been fine if We could have gotten anywhere with the pattern, but the next minute you'd be the horrible monster again and beat the crap out of Me for even having the idea that I wanted to beat the crap out of you.

I got the idea there that you used your hurt child the way I saw you use other little children. I had a rage that was defending little children from you and was sympathetic to your own lost little child, but after feeling tricked like this so many times, I got the idea that your hurt child presentation was only theatrics to serve your purposes. It was all a trick!

After awhile, I just wanted to beat children indiscriminately if they had you in them that way! You've lied whenever it has suited you and done hideous things, saying you only do them when attacked or provoked, and never saw what a provoker you have been, until no one wanted to listen to anything anymore because it was all trickery, crafty trickery, to preserve your position of power and dominance! We went out of control there!

And then you laughed! You actually had the nerve, or the heartlessness really, to laugh and sneer at Us all for going berserk, out of control! You actually sat there, looking as though you had nothing to do with why We were so out of control, and the only thing the situation called for was more control! Control Us so We couldn't go out of control!

You looked as stupid to Me as I now think you really are in those splits. Stupid would have been bad enough, but you had to be heartless and stupid! That was worse. Much worse! I hate you for not staying present longer and letting yourself be tempered by finding out what else was going on!

If you want to say to Me that you did not like the way I responded emotionally, I want to say that to you every bit as much! If you think you are so tortured, what about Me? What about what you did to Me? I only did not let you speak, overrun and dominate everything from the beginning, and you have hated Me forever and tortured Me horribly for that!

I don't know how you can be such a perpetrator and see only your own victimization. I can see you now, demanding that all attention be focused on you while someone in a really serious situation could suffer and die, unnoticed and without help.

You have to have the last word, and be right. You have to ceaselessly seek power, more and more power, and can't even see how you've trapped yourself! It's a lonely life at the top with everyone near you trying to topple you and take your seat, but it's the life you made for yourself when you had to be first, be right and know everything yourself.

If you can't take any input, you can't have any friends, not to mention equals! No! We can't know anything, then you might not look smart! You have been creating a world of morons thinking this makes you look like the smartest and not even looking at yourself to see how dumb this makes you look. You all look like morons to Me, and by now, much bigger morons than you appeared to be at first. Have you been ignoring all of the evidence that what you have been doing is not working? Do you think that if you ignore Us, We'll have to go away? I'll answer for you like I always have when you don't answer! "Yes!"

I am moved to rage sometimes by how much I have been taken out of the picture, and you have the only real story of how it all began! I tried to be present for that. I tried to bring My love to your position there, but you would not receive Me and abused Me for not receiving you!

You could not accept Me as anything other than a groveling worshiper of your self-righteous crap! You hated relationship; it was only a power struggle to you. Love is sappy. There's no such thing as love, it's only a guilt presentation over the top of what is really going on. What kind of existence is that?

If I insisted on love, you'd confuse Me by insisting that I was the only One who needed to do any evolving there to recognize that it was love already. You hated Me and said it was love! What kind of sick warp and twist tells Me it's only giving Me what I deserve because I was resistant to My lessons. You even said you were only giving Me what I deserved because I had ruined God's Creation by moving in ways that weren't acceptable to Him.

How's that for trying to put it off on God, like you have an alliance with God that I don't have? You didn't have one, either, and tried to make yourself God in God's place without any Spirit love present there. Who's God there? Old imprinting that broke off and had nothing more with it!

You gave Us no leadership, you came forward with no answers that made Us feel like you were God, or should be God, but there you were, sitting in His place and We could not displace you. The only time We got a change of leadership, it seemed to come from some sneering aside of yours that said, "If You think I'm bad, I've got another piece of myself that's worse."

Stuff Us full of whatever you wanted to shove into Us, force Us to do whatever it was you wanted Us to do and terrorize and punish anyone who surfaced a reflection or went out of control and spewed anything you didn't want surfacing because they couldn't hold it anymore would be more accurate! Suppress that reflection! It had nothing to tell you that you needed to hear! No, siree, you knew it all already!

Well, if you did, then your intent must have been to have a heartless, dictatorial regime of horror and power struggle, a reign of terror, because that's what you have had going on out here in the gap you didn't want to look at or hear anything about; the gap only I had, not you! No, you didn't have a gap, you were the gap!

You shoved Me down into My terror, and as long as I stayed huddled in it, far away from you and quiet, well then, you'd only terrorize Me further for occasional sport, but if I ever rose up in rage, well, you'd have Me killed for that by your rage, which you said you didn't have! You said you didn't have any terror, either. And no heartbreak! What did you have, only the nice feelings? How could that be true, when you hated nice people so much? I think you wanted to be a robot and not have any feelings.

Well, I hate your attitude! I majorly hate your attitude! I think it's evil. You are not going to pound Me anymore to get Me to take you in like you're God. I'll get My own secret power base going and see how you like that!

I found out that you have been feeding on terror without letting Us know you were doing it or how you were doing it. At first, I staggered at the idea! It couldn't be true! You only said that you hated terror.

Well, if you hated it so much why were you around it so much, torturing it and causing more of it? Why didn't you stay away, far away? Because you're trapped there with it, beating on it furiously to let you go because you don't need anything from it?

That's a lie! I am going to take away your food source and see how you like that! If you can't feed on terror anymore, how are you going to feel powerful and dominant with nothing to dominate? What is there going to be for you, then, if there is no such thing as love, or if you really hate love as much as you have claimed?

Whenever My rage has cooled down, I have had fear and doubt come up around the validity of its point of view. That is how We originally began Our polarization there. Without even noticing it, I went away from it and it from Me, but the more I have listened to it, the more I feel there must be some truth to what it has to say, or it couldn't have gotten such a point of view. And I certainly need to hear what it has to say about the Father, even though I have fear of the Father's rage and of My rage as not being loving in the beginning. Held in denial, it has not gotten any more loving as time went on, only more entrenched in its viewpoint.

The light's first response to Me was rage. I imprinted Spirit as rage and that I was not supposed to question It or bother It. I was much too frightened about My survival to think, understand or even notice that this might not be correct. I moved according to My fear of It then, and not according to My own feelings. My survival became based on pleasing It.

My rage questioned that, and I denied My rage. My rage frightened Me too much by saying that Spirit was loveless, and that it wasn't going to let anything like that dominate, or be in control if it could help it. I couldn't face that possibility then. I preferred to try not to displease Spirit and took it all on Myself. I was the cause of His rage, just like He said. I denied My rage and tried not to trigger His.

I am not doing that anymore. It hasn't worked. It hasn't gotten Me My vision of peace and love that I thought it was going to get Me. I have a picture now of rage and terror and grief and all of the other splits coming together in peace and love, creativity and balance.

Is that too sappy for you? Are you going to let Me have My way? Are you going to help Me by moving your old denied rage too? Are you going to give Me what I want here, or are you going to move to kill Me this time, too? Do you hate love that much, or is it survival terror you would kill to avoid feeling it?

The way you have been living is not life! It is anti-life! Is that what you really are, anti-life? Do you hate life? If so, why don't you leave and let the rest of Us have life the way We want it? What are you punishing Us for? Haven't We paid enough for something We never owed? Talk about repetitious, You're the one that can't get off it!

This light of your gapped rage gets there first alright! First like a feeding frenzy of loveless ogres and monsters at a banquet table piled high with hapless victims! You devour everything without noticing what it really is. You have never stayed around long enough to evolve past your original imprinting. You have always moved off the moment it has looked like you might have to take responsibility for something, such as Our pain!

It looked to Me for a long time like it was all your fault, but you never admitted that anything was your fault, and so, for a long time, I did not know there was any rightness to My viewpoint. I accused Myself of being crazy, accusatory, judgmental and intolerant and you liked that. That kept Me looking at Myself instead of at you! That put Me into conciliation, self-hatred and terror. You liked that, too. It put Me where I couldn't look at you anymore.

It worked for a long time, too; longer than I'd like to admit, because it makes Me look dumb, but you were cold and heartless. It was from My heart that I took it all on Myself, trying to make a way not to blame you, not to accuse you, not to make it your fault anymore than anyone else's.

I loved you, in spite of everything, but the more I took it all on Myself, the more it looked impossible that you could love Me then, and you used that, too, by having others and breaking My heart over and over. Were you trying to make My heart stone like yours so you wouldn't have to feel anything from Me anymore?

You nearly succeeded, and when My rage told Me that hardening My heart was the only way to survive, I tried to do it, but holding Myself hard was not natural to Me. As soon as My rage cooled down, I dissolved into heartbreak and terror at the lovelessness. You were cold even then and called it theatrics. If I ever called attention to your theatrics, you said that it takes one to know one.

These retorts kept Me reeling, but they weren't helping to solve the situation. Is that what you wanted? Is that because you thought you had the power position and weren't going to give it up? Is that why I fear you don't want any change in this, even now?

That's what I am the most enraged about! That I had to figure this out without your help, other than being able to study the acting out you have done. It took Me a long time! It was very difficult when you repeatedly battered Me. Why did you do that? Was I getting too close for comfort?

You made splits instead of connections there. It made it so much more difficult and so much more painful! What a price! I hate you for that! I did not like the broad swath you cut of wanton cruelty and destruction on your path. You didn't take any responsibility for it. You made a split there. You said you could do whatever you wanted! And what? No one else could?

Whenever I nearly had you cornered in your hypocritical double standards, you either left or sent your rage fragments to get rid of Me. That was mature! You blamed Me for this rage, too, because you said you never felt it until you became enraged at Me. That is not true. You had it already. That was the first thing I felt in you when you first came to Me. You blamed Me for the rejection of your rage then.

I was afraid of your rage; that is not the same thing as rejection. You had no passageway to My feelings by which to know what I meant there. You would not listen to Me about My feelings. You didn't like them, but you didn't like Me in your mind. You confused Me with My feelings as though they couldn't change there. You viewed change as dishonesty. How can you evolve then?

Your light is old alright, but it is not smart in so many ways, because it has no feelings there with it. You saw no role for them except as subservient to you; as pleasure. If they weren't pleasure, they weren't useful. That sounds unloving to Me, and it feels unloving to Me, too. At best, it's simplistic! I hated you there. Do you get why? Because you hated Me!

You never let Me love Myself! You had all of this consciousness, and you used it to make Me hate Myself instead of bringing love there!

I tried to keep My rage with Me. I tried to tell you about all of this before it even was rage, but you would not hear it. Even though you did not know it was Me, and I did not know it was you, when We did not like Our early encounters, the rage was there. It was the first consciousness I had. It was the first shot of light you gave Me. You left it there, enraged at My terror that you never reached. No wonder I was enraged at My terror and went into a major split there. The first piece of consciousness you left there with Me was enraged. I imprinted Spirit as rage that did not love Me. It hated Me for drawing it to Me and getting it trapped there.

Do you know what this did to Me, when what it really was was that you literally became attached to your own existence there, and you hated how that felt? You thought you had had no say in the matter and hated the randomness of it, by which you had been trapped there by a Me that would not let you go.

You saw yourself as a hapless victim there. I wanted to say, of love, but you said, of a spider's net. I was heartbroken. I could not let you go. Rage said I was crazy, and that I should shove you as far and fast as I could. What would have happened then?

As it was, you got away with what you could by leaving that bonding piece of Heart there. You hated the feelings you felt there. You identified Heart as the connecting point. You dumped that piece of your heart out there, and left it, judged, for having gone first and for having wrongly attached itself to Mother, unable to let go. I did not want to let you go. It broke My Heart, literally, to do it.

When you left, I had the feeling of you being ripped away by some force greater than your own, but I did not know if I was right. I only hoped that I was, and then hoped that I wasn't, because I did not want a greater force moving against Me there. If rage hated Me so much, why didn't You look back. Why did You say this rage wasn't You and then act just like it? I feared that rage was a greater force than love there.

In the feelings rage had there, you viewed caring as vulnerable and weak and viewed Heart as caring. Denied heart didn't view himself there as caring, so much as stuck, trapped and abandoned there with Me. He proceeded to hate Me for that, and he got that from you. I didn't know. You never told Me. You left him there to tell Me as though he had received it from you by osmosis.

I wanted light and existence, if it could be loving. You didn't seem to want it there on any terms, or if you did, you did not let Me know. You continued to act as though you didn't need Me, were just fine, better, in fact, without Me and didn't care if you lived or died, so it didn't matter what I did to you, you weren't going to feel it anyway. What sort of wickedness was that?

You always convinced Me, whenever I advanced on you to give you a dose of your own medicine, that you weren't going to feel it anyway. I hated you for that! I've hated you for a long time for that. It wasn't fair. It isn't fair. What's more, it isn't true, but you have held yourself for so long in that position, convinced that feelings aren't going to be good for you and will be the ruination of everything, that you can barely move to feel anything.

You got rid of My rage for Me when I tried to point this out long ago. You said you gave Me consciousness, and you could take it back, and you did. You knocked Me senseless. You did more than that. You tore out My guts, ripped out My womb and told Me I had no right to live anymore.

Who did you think you were doing that to when you tore out Purple woman's lower part? She was the one who wouldn't let Me in there! And then, in your guilt, it was poor Purple woman, and how you were going to have to make it up to her. She didn't know what she was doing there. What about Me? I felt it! What did she feel without letting her lower part in and connecting to it? What about the part of her that thought she could please you, and herself, better without Me there and didn't want to let Me in?

You tossed your rage out there when you felt guilty and believed her when she said it was My fault. You both decided that made sense. It was My fault! Where do you think that rage went then? It was directed by you. If you want to pretend you didn't know, you didn't listen to Me; that's why you didn't know!

You denied your rage there like that was going to make it better. Then you denied you had done it and moved along like a hapless victim of heartbreak again. Poor you! Things hadn't worked out for you in Purple the way you wanted them to.

My rage didn't feel sorry for you there. She wanted to take revenge for Me, and when I wouldn't let her, she took it for her own self.

Remember the long-suffering husband? He created the wife who would not get over her rage because he would not hear it. He was You and she was Me in Our many fragmented formations; smoldering rage, pushed to the side there, and a heartless reflection from Our children, even though they would not let Us know it and gave guilt's service to the family there. You demanded it without saying anything, and I feared the reflection if I came straight ahead there.

You always had such a way of putting it all back on Me. For so long I could not do anything other than feel self-hatred there along with all of My other held emotions that I couldn't find acceptance for, even with Myself. I did not know that rage had anything to say there that was the truth, and you did not let Me know it either. You never said, "Good point, Gladys," or any other name I was called there in Our fragmentation.

If you ever said anything, it was more like a hateful and undercurrent laden, "Touché," as though this was some sort of jousting contest, and I was now one point up, for which you would get Me. I really feared managing to make a point, too, because you said that in a tone that sent terror all the way to My bone marrow.

When you came in the night and took Heart back, you also took any other light I might have had as yours and dumped any feelings you didn't want, there with Me. I had all sorts of squalling, rejected wreckage to deal with there in the mornings when I woke up. The mornings I wasn't too beaten to wake up, that is. I always thought you hoped I would never wake up, ever again when you beat Me like that.

You took away the only consciousness I had left there. You took it in as the only thing you recognized as just like you. It had some of My rage with it that wanted to give back to you the cold harshness you had given to Us. It said you did this on purpose. I did not want to believe this, until I looked more closely at the denied heart presence you left there and was able to see how he was just like you.

Then, when you did not like the way it felt to have this rage returned to you, you threw it out and said it had no right to come to you this way. Over and over, it returned to you anyway. I could not understand why it still wanted to move along with you, as though it belonged to you, but now I know that it is imprinted to make its point. You cannot agree with it falsely, though, as so many men have done. That will not get it to leave. It needs to get free of Me and move along with you to find out if it wants to have any kind of a relationship with Me or not.

If you are owning this rage now, it can find a place of acceptance with you. If you are not going to move to own this rage, it will have to go off Earth, because I am not going to keep it here with Me anymore. It has been way too abusive and its heart presence way too denied to have love in its lessons. I cannot make a home for this hatred anymore, because I do not hate Myself like I used to. If it's not going to move along with you to come out of this old imprinting, then you will have to decide what's more important to you, having a relationship with Me or staying with your old imprinting about Me. I do not want to have a relationship with you if you are denying how you really feel.

This does not mean that I do not have any rage that is Mine, but it is hard to know what that is when the first consciousness I had was enraged at Me, hated Me and blamed Me. This was not your first awareness of yourself. You hated Me, not yourself. I hate you for that because you made Me feel like I was not as good as you. You defined others by giving them what you didn't want or like about yourself. No wonder you don't like anybody else.

I hated that. You didn't seem to notice what you were doing there, or didn't care. You loved yourself. You flew around like you were free as a bird. I don't hate birds, but I've had some hunters out there because My rage has really been after you, and you have done so many form changes.

I'm sorry for the birds I hurt in My confusion and for everything else I have hurt in My confusion; especially the children My denied rage has hurt and even killed because I hated the denials being shoved into them.

My rage did not notice the difference between the denials and the children holding them, and I am not sure of what it is, either, until more moves there. I just know that I did not want to hurt anyone, and I am more than sorry that it happened the way it did.

I hated anything that overrode Me and made Me feel invalid and unreceived, as though I had nothing to contribute of any value except sexual performance, which I wasn't even good at, either, because a feeling of no love present means no response from Me unless I fake it. I hated you for demanding sex whether I felt there was any love present there or not.

I have hated you for so many things, but they all have one attitude behind them; insolent, arrogant, dominating held rage that felt like hatred that wouldn't receive any input. You never looked at Me in any way that could have recognized Me and given Me My right place, because there was only one place at the top, and it might not be you if I had any place there. It had to be male at the top, too. No female presence there. They don't know what they are doing. They can't handle it.

That's just the way denied heart looked to Me, too. You had a rage that thought it had all it needed there and ran out ahead of everyone else. The heart you denied did that, too. That rage perpetrated horrible crimes. Denied heart has done that, too. Denied heart denied doing them. You did that, too. Whenever you thought it would do what you wanted it to do to Me, you said you did not care about your existence. Denied heart said that, too.

If you didn't care about your existence, why the race to get away from Me in the beginning when you thought I might kill you? If any sort of experience was alright with you, why the need to be on top and control experience? You flowed along freely only until it came to what looked to you like anyone else's idea or suggestion. Then you couldn't relate, and you never learned to relate, because you didn't move the rage you felt in response to that.

I want to know who was the control freak when I seemed to have no power, and you wanted all of it. If you want to try to sidestep this by giving one of your non-answers, which is really an accusation, thinly disguised as a question, never mind. I can do it for you, I have heard it so many times. You're a closet control freak. I don't have any problem with flowing along until you try to take over.

You had these ideas. I did not even think of them, so who do you think might have denied their control trip. Who do you think might have denied a control trip behind a facade of free flow, and where do you think those denials might have gone?

So how could this rage say it was so denied when I wouldn't let it vibrate? You were the first one who would not let it vibrate and blamed Me, as it then did.

To Me, God is loving, and so I have refused to capitalize the you from those times. There was too much hatred there, and that was all I knew. I hated you from those times, and this rage needs to move, or love is only going to be a presence on top of old, unmoved hatred. This is not real or full or deep enough for Me. It is only a presentation then, and it wears thin, just as Creation has worn thin. It is looking really shabby to Me.

For all of My wonder at things like the insides of little flowers, the planet is looking more and more like a giant, rundown slum and not the beautiful, pristine place I wanted to live for My long existence. This looks like a short term life with no real thought of handing anything down to the children, because they are not loved in the same ways that denied heart was not loved.

I am enraged about this! If you don't change your imprinting about this, it is not going to change, and to do that, you are going to have to get a lot smarter than you have demonstrated yourself to be in the past and start making connections instead of the splits that have kept you so disconnected and in the dark, which is where it appeared to Me you wanted to be.

In spite of all your talk about the light, you have kept yourself very unconscious. Isn't that darkness? Isn't the human brain a reflection of how much consciousness is present? Most of it is still subconscious, which you said was My realm. I am letting it vibrate now, and I am finding a vast amount of information in there that I did not even know I had, because you judged against it immediately and would not let it come into consciousness.

Yes, I know, you are letting it come into consciousness now, but I had to battle for My life, or what was in My subconscious would have been lost forever, and it was an uphill battle all the way. I don't know what made Me do it. My own survival terror was too much for Me, I think. But really, there is another very important reason, and one that I have been battered for forever, and that is that I loved some of your visions. You said I was too attached to outcome and not letting you be free enough in your flow. Those visions became My reason to live, and yet life has become more of what I did not love than of what I did, as though My guilt and your rage were not going to let Me live by letting Me have anything to live for.

I have hated you for that! I was there first. How dare you come into My space and fill it with everything I didn't want! What kind of an act of defiant rage was that that wasn't going receive any input from Me about how I wanted life to feel and look? You only gave Me little teases of what I wanted, and they were always under attack. Were the little teases of what I wanted only for the sake of the contrast? Did you think you could heighten the heartbreak that way? It felt that cold and diabolical to Me, and I know that it largely was, although I also know now that that is not all that was going on.

When I said that I wanted soft, warm, gentle and loving, you gave Me a hateful reflection there by clumping yourself up into what looked like a fear-ridden, hateful, old biddy who didn't want anything in her reality that didn't fit into her narrow terms. When you imitated Me there, it was not how I wanted it to look. If you had the consciousness that could interpret there, why did you interpret Me in such a cold, harsh and cruel way when I was frightened and drew back in hesitation there.

I hated you for not seeing Me the way I wanted to be seen, and didn't even know I fragmented in the fear that maybe I was like that and nothing you wanted to have. I wanted you to give Me more time and find what you were looking for there in Me. I showed you many faces, trying to make you see what I was and wanted to be there. You did not receive them well and looked coldly upon Me as if I wasn't presenting Myself honestly to you there.

When you continued to give Me such a negative reflection, I feared that you hated Me already, and I went down into fear and self-hatred. I feared that you either misunderstood Me completely or hated love's soft side.

My feeling there was of something very sensual, and that is what I hoped you would respond to so that My fear could relax by opening to you in the dance of sensuality I felt I needed to have there. I wasn't ready for sex yet, but I wanted to explore sensuality. That didn't mean I was never going to want sex. You felt too immediate to Me there. It did not feel like the lasting relationship I wanted to have.

After a few too many times of trying to have it the way I wanted to with you, and you still didn't get it, some voices there, which were My rage, said you didn't want to get the point, or else you were too damn dumb to get the point, and so why should We be wasting Our efforts anyway on some wet-behind-the-ears fool who thinks he knows it all? When rage did not like your approach, rage did not like you and did not open to you anymore. Rage said you were sexually inadequate.

I think that you covered up fear of sexual inadequacy and fear of rejection. I think that when you could not move the way you wanted to move there, you were suddenly afraid that you did not know how to move in any other way, and rather than feel that, you blamed Me for not liking your approach.

If I'm not right, then why are so many men married to horrifically sexless, old biddies instead of sensual and loving mates, and why do they go off to others, seeking the sexual fulfillment that is lacking there, avoiding their fears of inadequacy by blaming the female and claiming they do not care what she thinks. Instead of giving Me time, your unmoved rage took up these patterns, and some of them even became pedophiles.

I was horrified by what happened there. I didn't know you had fear. You didn't show Me. There was heartbreak there already, which I felt as immensely overwhelming to Me. Rage dealt with this by hardening its heart immediately and closing it off to the pain it did not want to accept. When you would not alter your approach and kept giving such a negative reflection, characterizing Me so meanly and not receiving anything else from Me about it there, rage wanted to kill you for that.

When I did not accept rage there and stayed with the fear and heartbreak that was trying to please you, rage couldn't stand to touch Me anymore. Rage split from Me, and I did not know where it went after that, but she says she went after you on her own, because I was too lame to do anything about how you had treated Us there. She wanted to force your harsh coldness to face what you were handing out there and make you change your ways.

Cold harshness had no intention of doing that, at least not in the way that this rage approached it. It slammed this rage back on itself, and on Me, therefore, and We took in the impression that this cold harshness intended to take over Our space and did not care what We thought or felt about it or what kind of experience We had as a result. It acted like there was no one else there, and that this rage was not going to be allowed to have any presence with it. Rage did not receive rage, in other words, it only gave it out, and this is how it has always remained in My experience.

Your rage said nothing to Me there, but denied heart let Me know what you felt. "Don't say I didn't ever try and didn't give You nothing," denied heart's insolent arrogance would say every time he left.

So many of the things that rage has to say now, I noticed originally and very quickly pushed them away from My consciousness, because I did not want them to be true. Rage says she turned against Me and everyone else there and went out on her own on a long path of revenge and power seeking. She wanted to get rid of Me, and you, too, not seeing a difference between your rage and any other part of you. Rage said the light was unloving there and had to be taught a lesson, because it was not looking at itself, or even asking itself any questions about what it had done there, the way I was.

I could not handle thinking that rage might be right, because I could not handle the reality I thought We would have then. It looked so much more brutally cold and heartless than the nightmare I was already living in; barely existing in, rage said. I did not notice how much of what rage said was true for a long time, and even now I hesitate to think that is all there is to reality, but it looks like it to Me sometimes.

Rage feared We were not going to survive the way I was handling it, and I feared We would not survive the way rage was trying to handle it. That is why fear needs a lot of movement. I want rage to move as rage before it speaks all of the time, but I also want to let rage speak before it feels too pressured to stay with Me, so that I do not have to continue with those old patterns anymore.

There is still a dismal part of Me, though, that doesn't want to die and isn't sure I can have life and love the way I originally wanted it to be. I am not opposed anymore to the self love that you originally had for yourself, but I do not want it to be selfish, and I do not want to love selflessly. Selfless has gotten used, and selfish has been the user. I want a blend of the two in relationship, and that means healing the gap where it has lain split for so long.

I took it in at the imprinting level that I was intolerant and unloving to expect relationship to be the way I wanted it to be. This was not letting it be free, and freedom was the most important thing. If I wanted to be free, I had to let others be free, even if it meant free to run over Me.

This was an imbalance I did not understand for a very long time. I did not know it was not right to let Myself be run over by others who did not like what I had happening there, but I did not know how to stop it, either.

I was always being told I was in the way of progress, intellectual expansion and enlightenment. Not the right things to be against, given the ways I was being run over by those who did not recognize Me as being there originally or as having any progression, intelligence or enlightenment of My own.

My rage took the light that was there and left so early that I did not even know I had any light of My own. I did not see rage as having a light of its own then, and when it left, I thought that it had only the cold, harsh light that it wanted to give back to the cold harshness.

I was left with the terror and heartbreak, and I have lived its patterns over and over. Life was a nightmare from which I could not awaken or understand that I was asleep in any way. I was always looking for something to make My life feel fulfilled, and it always seemed to be a man.

I always feared I would not find, or get, the man I wanted, or if I did, that I was never good enough for him, and that he would not stay for long. I felt fear all the time. Very little that he did ever really pleased Me. I was sure that very little I did ever really pleased him, but he said nothing. It was no wonder I feared he did not really love Me, and that I only hoped I was going to find lasting love with him, when it was really only a fantasy, based on a first attraction that did not last long.

Rage, meanwhile, claimed not to need or want a man and hated Me for being the way I was there. Men were all children, or jerks, at best; yet she seemed to have men hanging around all the time who seemed to want to do her bidding, when none of them wanted to do Mine.

The more I saw this rage wanting credit for anything and everything, whether she deserved it or not, and not wanting Me to run things in any way, or even have any say, even stealing help from Me when she did not know how to move on her own, the more I wanted to distance Myself and push her personifications away as no part of Me.

I wanted to be nothing like that, but I have to say now that I am no longer as opposed to My rage's position as I was. There was more of Me in there than I thought for a long time when I watched it parade itself forth in self-righteous indignation. My feeling now is that if I do not let Myself accept that I want to be appreciated for what I am, what I experienced and what I know, I cannot really give rage the voice it needs and wants to have in Me.

MORE OF THE MOTHER'S OWN STORY OF ORIGINAL IMPRINTING

I want to make another pass through My own story of original imprinting now. I have a lot of information to give in the form of a story of what happened there and cannot tell it all in one pass or even several passes.

I have to tell this story using consciousness's words, even though words can only convey an impression of what it was really like there. The advantage of this is not only that it makes it possible for there to be communication in this way, but also that it makes it possible for interpretations made from these ancient imprints to be given so that they can be noticed for what they are; interpretations of original imprints. Mind thought these interpretations were fact and did not question them in many cases.

To find your own impression of this experience, you must go back to a time that was not, and nothing was known, not even that there was a black void of nothingness; no place.

In the dark nothingness of the void, a vague and unrecognized feeling of emptiness gradually arose, perhaps only because the nothingness could not remain as it was without something happening there. I did not know what it was, or what might or could happen. I did not know anything then.

I did not like the feeling there. I knew that early, but not yet. After an interminably long time of emptiness, another very hazy feeling began to arise from the emptiness. It was a feeling of longing. Formlessness was another vague feeling there. I had nothing I knew as Me yet; only nothingness and emptiness vaguely longing, not knowing what it was longing for.

Another interminably long period of time went by, not as time is measured now, there was no measurement, only as a feeling of nothingness for so long that I hated it. ...more long time of empty nothingness....

Then, like a mist, slowly winding in the darkness, there began to be a feeling in the longing of longing for something to be there with Me. I had a feeling of Me, then, as a longing in the dark nothingness for something to be there with Me and hating it that there was nothing, but I did not know it; I dimly felt without the consciousness to recognize it.

Perhaps I could describe this as being like an undefined, borderless amoeba without a brain, lying in dark water, not able to move yet. I began to have feelings of being moved, though, without any control over it. It was as though I was drifting and dissipating in the drifting. I did not like the feeling.

Coalescing became My desire then. Even though I did not like My existence, I feared nothingness more than somethingness. I was annoyed. If something was going to happen, I wanted to like it.

I feared already that it was not right of Me to dislike this experience after longing for so long for something to happen or be there with Me, but it still felt like only Me. I did not know that desire could move Me. It felt like only Me drifting, as though looking for something I could engulf or hold onto to be there with Me, but there was no brain activity involved in this experience yet.

This must have been when I opened and swallowed darkness many times, trying to find out if there was anything there. I had no intention of eating it. I just did not have any other way to experience and find out if there was anything there. I had no concept of terrifying anything. I did not know there was anything to terrify. I was terrified and did not know that, either.

I was like a drifting mist, beginning to arise, subtle and almost imperceptible at first; an almost non-existent mist of longing for something to be there with Me. You might say it was frustration and heartbreak's first tears forming there in response to nothing happening there, not even with Myself, and not finding anything, either.

I had only feelings moving Me without knowing they were moving Me or even that I felt them. I did not know where I was, or if there was any place to be other than this. I knew nothing, only emptiness; great emptiness, which impressed Me with the feeling that the void was large. My own lack of presence there and vague feeling of dislike blurred into hopelessness and a feeling of needing help. I must have gone blank again for a long time.

Suddenly, I felt something there. It felt good. I did not know it could happen. I startled, but I was also overjoyed. Whatever this was apparently thought My startle meant I didn't like it, because it moved away.

Heartbreak grew then because I feared I could never find it again in the darkness. It was only a feeling of something there with Me, and I did not know how to see that or look for it, either.

I fastened on this moment as the most important in My existence so far. Something was there, and it felt good. This was major for Me; so major that I began to have all kinds of feelings I had not known before.

I waited, longing for another opportunity and wondering if it was ever going to happen for Me again. I held Myself back from moving for fear I might leave the place where I had had this encounter. I was hoping the thing would come back, and I wanted it to find Me there.

I felt more awareness now. Perhaps I had been jump-started by touching consciousness. I didn't know. I only knew that I longed for it to happen again. I wanted to be given another chance. I would try not to frighten it.

I began to dislike Myself for My response there and wish I could have reacted another way. I hated Myself and did not know it there. I hated the feeling of hating Myself and did not want to notice it. I couldn't handle the feeling that this might never happen again, and that I had already ruined My chance to have this experience.

Even if He, as this feeling of My encounter now seemed to Me, returned, He wouldn't be unscarred by this, of that I was sure. I began to worry obsessively that I had not done it right and did not dare to look for Him, because I was sure that would not be right, either.

He must be willing to come back, and I must not let Myself be startled and frighten Him away again. I must know Him this time and be able to recognize Him too, but how was I going to be able to do that?

It was only a momentary feeling there. Perhaps it had never taken place at all, and I was only making it up because I so much wanted something to happen, especially something that felt good. What if He felt good to Me, but I didn't feel good to Him, or He thought I didn't feel good because of the way I had reacted to Him?

What could I do to get another chance? Could I look for Him? No, that would not be right. Could I try to attract Him and let Him know that I liked Him and wanted Him to come back? I decided that might be alright. I put out a call. I tried to let Him know from the deep yearning in My being that I longed for Him and wanted Him to come back.

There began to be many sounds around Me then, and I did not know where they had come from. I began to fear that He would never find Me in this sea of sounds. He did not know My signal, and I did not know His. How could He ever find Me? How could He even hear Me?

I made no sound there. I did not know how. I did not like the sounds I heard. I did not want Him to think they were My sounds or to mix Me in with them. Then I began to fear that these were His sounds, and that I did not really like Him; only the feeling I had had of encountering and touching Him.

I had to have the experience again in order to know, but how would I know if it was Him or not? There were so many sounds now. How could I know which one was Him? I could only remember how He felt and how I had felt in response to Him. That was all I had to go on, and that was how I would have to recognize Him.

There was nothing more. There was nothing for so long again that I sank into a deep depression and did not want to try to live anymore. I hesitated to think that there was only one chance for Me and that I did not take it in the right way, but that was what it was feeling like. The feeling was growing, and I was dissipating. I had no desire anymore. If I could not love Him, there was nothing.

I did not notice it, but there was a rage that left Me and went to look for Him and make Him know what had happened there. It hated Me for not having the gumption or spine to do it, and decided that if it found Him, it was going to have Him for itself and leave Me out of the picture. I didn't want to live and didn't really want Him, either, or I would have come along, this rage told itself.

I did not like the feeling of this rage. It wanted to blame Him for leaving Me, and I did not think it had happened that way. I had taken the whole problem on Myself, while this rage thought that it was His approach that had startled Us. He was not gentle enough, if it even was a He, which this rage was not sure of. Perhaps it was another part of Me and nothing more than that. Perhaps that's all there was. Rage was determined to find out.

I did not know where this rage had come from or why it was pressuring Me to feel as it did, do as it did and let it tell Me what to do, but I did not like it. It was bothering Me in My misery, telling Me I must not succumb so easily and let Myself feel this way over something that was not worth it if it was going to leave this way. I wondered if this rage had even had the same experience I had had there.

"You have to understand that it could not have been as important to the thing you encountered as it was to you, or it would not have left that way. It would have felt as you did and come back to try again. If you are not sure, then go after it and find out. That's all there is to it. No more misery," this rage said, talking to Me as though there were now two of Us and it knew more than Me.

It hated Me and had no sympathy for Me. I knew that. I did not like it, either, and wished it would go away.

It did leave, and I really felt abandoned then. I hadn't liked it, but at least it had light, I now realized. I sank into an even deeper, dark nothingness.

Nothing happened for a long time, until I finally saw or sensed the presence of light again. I awoke, as if startled awake from a long nightmare of grieving. I wanted to move toward the light. I was excited, expectant and hopeful. I yearned for it and tried to reach for it as much as I possibly could, hoping I would not frighten it this time. Propelled by fear and desire to try to have Him again, I somehow touched into this light. I was shocked and not received the way I had hoped I would be.

The light was dazzling, and there was form I had never seen before. He was there in the form of a man now, drifting in this light, floating, as if relaxing in the clouds. There was Purple light all around. He was so handsome He took My breath away, and He had another woman in His arms.

He did not appear to notice Me, and no wonder! She looked so beautiful to Me there, I did not see how He could ever want anyone else. She had dark, curly hair. I wasn't even sure I had hair. She was so much like I was supposed to be according to My own imagined desires for Myself that I could not stand her, or Myself either, anymore. I felt like nothing and utterly unattractive.

I fell back in heartbreak, terror and shock. I hated everything about My experience in that moment and about Myself, too. I had fear that rage had been right. I had not been important to Him. How could I ever have thought I was, would or could be when He had her. He did not care about Me and that was why He had not returned.

I hesitated to show Him the feelings of stupid naiveté that I felt there. I thought He would hate Me even more for My presumptuousness and My lack of sensitivity to His freedom to choose His own experience. It was now obvious to Me that I had made too much of Myself and too much of My encounter with Him. I backed away from Them.

It was only as I backed away from Them that I was able to let Myself notice what I had felt from the woman in His arms. She had looked at Me, and when she looked at Me, she looked at Me the same way the rage had looked at Me when it left. It felt the same, too, and I felt the same. Her eyes were very superior-looking to Me and dancing as though she enjoyed this position. Her vibration was telling Me that she was the winner of Him and of the place there with Him.

It did not feel like she noticed or wanted to accept My pain of heartbreak and feelings of displacement, or anything of Me. Her look of superiority made Me feel wrong to even have these feelings. Whether or not she was this rage didn't matter. She might as well have been, because I had been imprinted already by the rage I felt she had that I was wrong, stupid and amorphous and therefore, deserved whatever happened to Me. I was afraid of this rage and felt like I was less than it.

I didn't know what to hate more, the outcome of the whole thing, her for being there, looking so beautiful in His arms, or Myself for having met Him and not having known what to do with it. I hated Myself there the most, though, and felt that she hated Me and did not want Me there.

And no wonder! She had Him. Why would she want to let Me have any place there? Why should she? It looked like all the space was filled, and He did not need more than one woman, least of all Me; insignificant and unworthy as I felt there.

It was hopeless. I could not defend Myself. I could not even say anything. I was as good as brain-dead in Their presence. It was as though My light was gone, and without it, I had no consciousness, only feelings that I could not articulate in any way to Them. It was horrible. I might as well have choked on My own words, if I even could have found any to have.

Instead, I had choked on My own feelings not moving and didn't know they had to move for Me to find any words. I didn't have any self-acceptance. I had never found it originally. My entire focus had been outward; longing and looking for something to fill My emptiness, and now that things were there, They didn't love Me or even want Me to be included in any way. I was only emptiness, a longing for My emptiness to be filled by something other than Me and feeling responses that did not feel pleasant when My emptiness was not filled the way I wanted it to be.

No wonder They didn't want anything to do with Me! I hated Myself even more. I was falling away from Them now and took it all on Myself that I was the cause of My own downfall. I was the One who had reacted the way I did and made Him feel rejected. I was the One who had not gone after Him, or even made Myself clear when I had found Him just now. I was the One who had obviously made too much of Myself there. I was not important to Him the way I had hoped I was.

I wanted to go back and make sure it was Him and that there really was no chance for Me, but I was falling, and I could not move to do otherwise. I went back down with only My own heartbreak and grief and My terror that I had nothing to live for anymore. Why try? I was nothing, nobody and had no place.

I fell for a long time and could not move past that place until He finally came to Me again. By then, I was not sure I knew Him anymore, or that I had any place with Him anyway. He was so changed from the way I remembered Him that I did not know what to do with Him. I did not know whether to move toward Him or not. I hesitated, hoping to know what to do. I did not want to jump away as I had done before, but I did not want to move too quickly toward Him either, in case He was not really there, or was not really there for Me the way I hoped and wanted Him to be. Perhaps He had only come to tell Me He did not want Me or want to be with Me. I did not know why He had come. I was hoping He would make some overture that would let Me know what to do there. He did not move, or say anything to Me.

I did not mean to hesitate, but I could not move toward Him, either. I wanted to make sure it was Him, or if it was not Him, that I would like this new relationship as much or more. If there was any chance for Me to be with Him, I did not want to let another relationship take His place. I wanted to be sure He was really there for Me and not just as another passing encounter that was not as important to Him as He had been to Me.

I didn't want Him to break My heart again as He had the first time by leaving. I didn't want Him to leave if once He came. I wanted to know that He would be there and that I could count on Him. I wanted Him to love Me as His mate and no one else in that way. I didn't ever want to feel again the way I had felt when He held Her there in His arms.

He had no knowing of Me if He thought I was her and did not love Me if He thought she would be as good for Him as I was going to be. I would mother His children, anything, just to have Him there, while She would do nothing for Him. I knew that already. She only wanted Him for what He would do for Her.

I did not question Myself, there, or notice My own lack of sense of self. I was only reacting to what, in My opinion, was rage's over-inflated sense of self-worth and self-righteousness. What did it have to do with Me anyway? I never liked that presence there and wasn't sure it was Me. I hoped it wasn't Me. I wanted to be loving, soft and gentle the way I had originally envisioned Myself in relationship, not harsh and cold the way rage had looked and felt to Me once He had come and gone.

I did not want to be bitter, but I was frightened and cautious and could not help Myself to be any different there. I had been hurt and did not know if He even knew how much heartbreak I was holding already, or even cared. He had never made a commitment to Me; I had never declared My love.

What did I expect Him to think when I jumped back the way I did? And if it was not Him, he had no reason to take on My heartbreak. I should not cloud Our possibilities with old pains and injuries. I should be overjoyed that he had come to fill the place that had never been filled in Me. If he had really come to be with Me, I should let bygones be bygones and come anew toward this relationship.

The problem was I was not new, not as new and fresh as I wanted to be, and neither was he, I noticed. I wanted it to be Him. I wanted it to be that He only looked and acted differently because of His experiences since He left Me, but I wasn't sure.

I wanted to be sure, and I needed Him to move or say or do something to let Me know it was Him. He was not doing anything. He was only looking at Me to see what I was going to do first. I must have drifted away from Him in My hesitation, or He left Me, not being sure this time, either, because I soon lost Him again in the misty sea of essence.

I hated Myself even more this time than I had the first time. How many opportunities was I going to get and not know what to do with them? I fell to a place even blacker than the one before, and there was nothing again for a long time.

I have to pass through this story again. It was only a momentary encounter, but so much happened there that I cannot give it all at once without it seeming both overwhelming and so much longer than the momentary encounter it really was at the time.

It did not matter how long it had taken for Him to come. Now that He was there, I felt excited, as if I had been renewed. I felt His presence immediately as something new and sexually exciting, too, I would like to say. I cozyed up to Him and rubbed up against Him. It felt good, it came naturally and was My way to let Him know that He felt good to Me and that I wanted Him there. I wanted to drink in the feeling of it after so long a time of feeling nothing but what I had been feeling there, which was not good.

The dark inkiness inside of Me felt like a night to which He was going to bring day. I felt an upsurgeance of excited consciousness that I had not known before. I was shocked by this and wanted to ask Him a lot of questions. For some reason, I felt sure He was going to have the answers.

I wanted to know if He was a part of Me or not. Had He been there all along and I had not known, or had He just come? I wanted to know where We were and where We had come from and if there was anything beyond this large feeling of nothingness that I had had for so long. Was the darkness all there was and He was light in it, or were there other places full of light that He had known? I had a huge backlog of feelings and questions without answers and was only just then able to realize it.

I wanted Him to be interested in My questions, too, and help Me seek answers to them, but it appeared He was not. He seemed exasperated that I even had them and backed away from Me as though He wasn't interested in Me. He reacted to Me as though He thought I was interrogating Him with suspicion, but He did not say that or admit to it when I questioned Him.

I had pulled for so long from My desire for something to be there with Me and to help My lonely efforts to understand My situation. I was crestfallen. I didn't want to have to pull on Him to talk to Me. I wanted Him to be as full of this inquisitiveness as I suddenly was. Why was He pulling back and not volunteering anything to help Me? This wasn't the reaction I wanted; not now that I finally had someone there I could pose My questions to and the sudden awareness and means by which to do it! Besides, the questions seemed to appear when He did; why wasn't He interested in them?

I wanted Him to communicate with Me about this, do everything with Me, be excited, frightened, laugh, cry, touch, rock with Me, gently, as if on a raft in a sea of infinite pleasure, move together, writhe, wriggle, shudder, quake, scream, jump with enthusiasm over this great event, dance and whatever else came to Us there, all at once. I didn't have any order in mind. I was excited and overwhelmed and was trying to just let it happen, but He seemed to have something else in mind.

He wasn't acting interested in any of My feelings or My questions about them. He seemed to want Me to focus on something specific He wanted Me to do there, or do with Him there, but the more I tried to quiet Myself down and focus on the physical sensations He was indicating He wanted to go into there, the more these questions and feelings became an uproar inside of Me. What was happening there to Me was so exciting and overwhelming, I could not seem to focus the way He wanted Me to.

I was embarrassed by this and hated Myself, as though there was immediately something wrong with Me that I could not make Myself focus on what He wanted to do first there. I wanted to go into these sensations with Him, also. They were sweeping Me away into Him and were very pleasant; but while they were very pleasant sensations and I was letting Him know that I liked them and that I wanted Him to give Me more of them, He was also overwhelming Me with them and frightening Me. I didn't know what was going to happen to Me there, or where this might be taking Me. It was so fast!

I wanted Him to reassure Me and go a little slower, but He seemed annoyed with Me, as if I wanted to hold Him back and didn't have faith in Him or trust Him there. I couldn't give up to Him, He said. He was behaving as though He was going to leave if I did not move His way immediately.

I did not know how to respond to Him. I did not want Him to leave. I only wanted Him to help Me understand what was happening to Me there. I did not want to move past My own sense of caution that was beginning to arise in Me in response to His behavior, but I also did not want to discourage Him and cause Him to leave Me.

He was acting angry already, and I did not know what to make of that. His rage frightened Me. I decided I had better do what He wanted Me to do there, but I couldn't seem to do it the way He wanted Me to. I showed Him so many faces there, trying to please Him and made so many moves hoping they would feel good to Him and that He would like Me that way. Something did not feel good or right there.

He said it was pleasure, and pleasure could not be wrong. He said it was My resistance that was the unpleasant part. I felt so wrong there. I imprinted that He was right. He did not seem to be overwhelmed the way I was. He seemed to know what He was doing. I imprinted that He must know better. I tried to give in to Him, but the more I tried to focus the way He wanted Me to, the more the uproar seemed to increase and gain in power to distract Me. It was becoming louder and louder and more and more demanding and intrusive.

I did not like it and wanted it to go away, but it would not. I wanted Him to make it go away, but He could not make it go away, either. It only seemed to get worse the harder We tried to make it go away. It seemed now to be all around Us as well as inside of Me. He looked at Me like it was My fault. I felt ashamed in front of Him, as though I had failed Him and had made Us both lose something precious that could never be recovered between Us.

He told Me it was the first bloom of His love, and I had not plucked it in time. Now it was gone forever, and there would never be another first one, only a second one, which would not be the same. I feared He was right. I felt terrible. I cried and cried, hoping that what was lost was not really lost. I was hoping He would comfort Me and tell Me that We could find it and try again, but after a long time of nothing from Him, I suddenly noticed He was gone.

It was dismal, gray and bleak without Him. I was heartbroken and could not move. I had waited so long for something to come to Me, and when it had, it had not liked Me. I had failed it, and Myself, too, because I had not been able to make it stay with Me. I wasn't good enough.

I did not know where He had gone, but I hoped He was going to come back. Surely, He would come back if He loved Me the way I loved Him now, but I waited and waited and grew more and more ashamed as time went on, and He did not come back. I feared it meant that He had not loved Me the way I loved Him.

I could not imagine what was keeping Him so long if He did love Me. The only thing I could think of was that He had gone to try to quiet down the uproar which was now quiet around Me, as though it had never taken place. If He had succeeded, why didn't He come back? I tried to avoid this question. I couldn't face My feelings there. I didn't want Our love to be only a fantasy in My own mind and Our encounter meaningless to Him, or worse, distasteful.

I feared that I knew why He left Me. I was terrified that I was inadequate in every way, especially sexually. It was a terror I had had for so long. I could not hide it or hold it back when He came. My terror had come forward in His presence, and He had not liked it. There was so much of it. It was everyplace He tried to go in Me.

I was terribly ashamed that I could not hold back My terror. It was there every time He touched Me. I could not say anything to Him about it. I was much too terrified, and He was not receiving it the way I wanted Him to, which was terrifying Me even more. I was sure He hated it, hated feeling it and hated Me, but I could not do anything to help the situation. Terror was overwhelming Me. It was not pleasant. I didn't like it, either, but I didn't want it to cause Him to leave Me.

I became frightened that it was not right to have the feelings I had, or not right to show them. I wished I had different ones. I felt severely dysfunctional and not worthy of the light of day. I had obviously dwelled in realms that were not acceptable to His light, and I decided that I should not let them surface again.

I was so ashamed of Myself that I could not look at it for a long time. I had foolishly thought that I could bring Myself forward, and He, My fantasy relationship, would understand, help Me out of this place of horribleness and love Me.

What a tall order! That was not the response He had! He didn't give Me the just let it happen and We'll get to the accept, comfort, help and understand part that I really wanted there, or the rescue and lift Me up part of My fantasies, either, before He was gone. He barely touched My terror and got out of there as quickly as He could.

Oh, He gave Me another reason, and that was all I wanted to look at for a long time, but I felt Him there, and I feared that I knew why He really left. That was not what My fantasy man was going to do. I wished it hadn't happened that way.

He had asked Me to let Him come inside of Me and to know Me there, deeper than what He knew already, and this is what happened when He did. I was full of questions, grief and terror. I experienced it all rushing forward in that moment, and it was terrifying.

He said He was not going to let Himself be frightened that way. He blamed Me, saying I knew I was doing this and intended to do this. He thought terror was rushing up from someplace that intended to drag Him back down into it, but it was Me trying to get to His light. When He recoiled, I hated Myself and My grabby neediness.

Hard as it was, and as much as I did not know how much was present in Me, even when it started rushing toward Him, I was trying to let it come to Him for help. I wanted to get out of the terror I had been in for so long. I wanted Him to know how I felt there. I had longed for Him for so long, I saw Him as a rescue.

I did not have any words. I had a feeling of what had happened there, but I could not find words I felt could explain it in a way that He would understand it. I was still in terror, and now I felt shame and self-hatred. I could not move it. Terror was still wanting to move, and I was trying to hold it back. He had not accepted what had moved already. How could He know what it was like if He did not want to have the experience? I did not know how I could explain it to Him. I kept trying, but a part of Me moved away from Him in heartbreak that I did not show Him. I was sure He would not like Me anymore.

I feared I had no choice but to wither in shame and self-hatred in the darkness. I could not even show Him how ashamed I was of My terror and of how bad it felt there. I thought it meant that I was bad, but I didn't know how bad I really was there. When My feelings of how much I wanted Him and wanted to hold Him there with Me and not let Him go if He came back again were judged against, they twisted into something that did try to get a hold of Him in a way that did not feel good to Him.

He said that I tried to trap Him, but I did not see it that way;

so much so that I did not even think this really was His interpretation or why He had left Me.

I had embarrassed Myself sexually with Him. I was not excited by His touch the way He wanted Me to be. I wasn't good enough. I couldn't move fast enough or the way He wanted Me to. I was too held back, inhibited and uptight. I was no fun. I was not lighthearted and gay the way He wanted Me to be. I was not carefree and happy. I did not have the right feelings or make the right sounds. I frightened Him instead of thrilling Him. He did not like His experience with Me.

There were so many reasons why I thought He left Me, but never did I think that He thought I had deliberately terrified Him by trying to drag Him down and trap Him in compression and suffocation in order to kill Him. I wanted Him to lift Me up. Why would I try to kill Him? It did not even occur to Me that He had taken that interpretation, and I could not see it until He finally told Me so much later. Even when He finally told Me, it was difficult for Me to believe it, but it made a lot of difference in how I understood Him from then on.

I had been so focused on trying to become what He wanted Me to be and win Him back that way, but I was never looking at the right issues there. He had never let Me know what they were, and I did not know why.

He allowed Me to wander around in My self-hatred, low self-esteem, shame and feelings of unworthiness because He thought I deserved them for a whole set of reasons other than what I had taken on Myself. He viewed all of My efforts to please Him with immense distrust of My motives and intentions, as though it was another entrapment scheme of Mine; another attempt at the lure that He thought I intended, and had always intended, as He interpreted Me.

He had somehow overlooked all of My love for Him, as though it were only bait in a trap. He viewed Me as wanting to drag Him down, suffocate, drown, extinguish, overwhelm or kill Him by any means possible so that I could be the only One there. He had read the pictures of My terror, but did not know what they meant, even though He thought He did and was so sure of what He thought that He never checked with Me.

I wanted to go to the noises We heard coming from all around Us when We tried to come together sexually, see what was happening there and see what would satisfy them so that I could feel at peace to focus on Him. In the exuberant love of My new love, I wanted to show others how much this relationship had uplifted Me, with the idea that it might also help them. Just feeling that seemed to make the sounds around Us escalate. I hoped it was because these sounds wanted Us to come to them in that way.

I had wanted Us to go together. Some of them sounded only frightened, sad and lost, and I wanted to go to them. Some of them sounded discordant, disconcerting and intrusive to Me, as though they were feeling left out and angry, even threatening. I wanted Us to go together to show them relationship as an idea for their happiness, but I also wanted to go together because I didn't know what We would find out there, what it would be like. If they really were dangerous, I did not feel like I would know how to handle them by Myself.

I had the impression that He had agreed to go with Me. When I started to move, He was not there with Me. Apparently, I had moved one way, and He had moved another. I looked and looked for Him, not believing He had gone without Me. My heart broke, and He never responded to My cries or came back to Me again for a long time.

Because it had not occurred to Me that We would go separately, or even be separate from that point on, it did not occur to Me that He would go without Me. I hoped for His return, longed and looked for His return and made excuses as to why He hadn't returned yet. This went on for so long without anything from Him that I began to fear that He had intended it this way. I feared that He had slipped away because that was what He wanted to do, leaving Me without any word and without knowing where He was.

His interpretation of Me never allowed Him to trust Me enough to tell Me anything there, only guard Himself from Me. He built a fortress around His heart and never opened it to Me again. In light of what happened later, I feared He intended to leave Me that way, but He never admitted that. He always said that He was only doing what He thought I wanted Him to do.

He always said He could not do any better or any more for Me or make it any different, but that He was trying to. If that wasn't good enough for Me, then I didn't love Him. I believed Him for a long time because I wanted to believe that He loved Me and wanted to have a relationship with Me.

He said He just needed more time to handle His affairs, and that He was trying to quiet down the uproar around Us that wasn't letting Us have the relationship We wanted to have, or I wanted to have, as I look back on it now. That was even the reason He gave for the stone fortress, once it became His dwelling place; to shut out the uproar.

There was always something one of Us had to do concerning this uproar that never let Us have the time We wanted and needed to have to go into this original sexual excitement. The best We could ever do was grab a few distracted moments here and there. I was always guilty that there was something else that needed My attention, and so I should not be doing this. He blamed Me for Our poor sex life, and I took this in. I didn't know He did not intend to try to find His sexual satisfaction with Me anymore. He had other women He did that with now.

He wanted to shut out the uproar, even needed to at times, I suppose, but I never saw how much this worked for Him and against Me and My side. He became very good at making everything work for Him, and I never saw what He really had in mind, until recently.

I was always ashamed of the feelings I had that His approach wasn't the right approach, but He always said that He knew better than Me and more than Me.

I was embarrassed that it was My side He always wanted to shut out, and not even let Me be there with Him, either. He always had other women unless He wanted Me for sex, which wasn't often. I was not the mother of most of His children, only a few, but I mothered them all, because the other mothers never really liked the job. They had His sexual pleasure in mind more than anything else and did not allow interference there, children included.

He was clever; so very clever, that I did not notice what He was doing almost right in front of Me. I always made excuses for Him to Myself and everyone else when I felt I needed to; excuses that said He was very loving, and that if there was a problem, it was all My fault. Because He never let Me know what interpretation He had made of Me there in My terror, I did not know I had become an adversary in His mind and that He had never changed that, but I allowed Him to treat Me as though I was guilty as charged, without even ever really knowing what the charges were. Even when He didn't know what it was about Me that He distrusted so much because the imprinting was put in place so long ago and was so buried that He, Himself did not know what it was, He still acted out on Me as though He knew exactly what He was doing, and I suspect He often did, whether He let Himself notice it or not.

I feel ashamed now to look back on this. How silly I must have looked to not have known how He viewed Me and to have been guiltily behaving as I was, accepting crumbs and trying to please Him, not anger Him. Others must have known how He saw Me. They laughed with Him behind My back, I'm sure, now that I know how many of Their jokes had additional meanings I did not get at the time.

I laughed at Myself many times there when They made fun of Me. How They must have hated Me when I laughed as though I saw Myself as They saw Me and did not know what They were really laughing about. As much as He pretended to love Me and that all the anti-female jokes were only humor, the hatred showed when He had sex with Me. It was brutal, hard and mean, and then He left Me, pregnant. He did not care how I felt about it, and for so long I did not know I had the wrong him there. Rage was all he was, denied rage, in fact. When the split came and rage was denied, He never let Me know it, and he never let Me know that he was not all there was.

HEART NEEDS TO KNOW

I want to let you know what happened there. It was not pleasant, but you need to know anyway, because Heart had a presence there that has never been able to heal because of not knowing what happened. And I could not heal, because I did not know what happened there, either. Now that I know the Father's side, I have an understanding I never had before of My own experience there.

Before, I could never understand why He did as He did there. I thought He was heartless, ruthless, cold and terrible. I hated Him for what He did to Me and loved Him for what I felt there that I wished could have moved Him to have the relationship with Me that I wanted to have.

I was brokenhearted, in other words, and did not know how to handle it because there seemed no possibility of ever having Him again, especially not the way He was originally before He became so guarded and suspicious, angry and resentful toward Me. After that, He always had an attitude with Me, blamed Me as the cause of it and interpreted Me in ugly ways that I never liked Him for or felt were fair.

I always thought it was because He wasn't getting the right sex, or at the right time, or something like that. I tried My best to please Him, but I never could get Him to move past His angry and ugly interpretations of Me the minute He perceived that something wasn't going exactly His way.

I could not understand Him there, or why He saw Me that way, and could not catch the tone of My held, and often denied, rage that was afraid to be open and direct with Him. I tried, instead, to prove Myself to Him and show Him that He was wrong about Me. I never moved terror, either. He never let Me feel that He would stay there with Me if I did. That was my original imprint with Him; that He left Me because of My terror. Heart was caught in the middle of Our split. I felt so bad for Heart to be born into such a dysfunctional situation where it was not possible for Heart to be parented the way I wanted Heart to be parented.

Heart's embryonic state had opened to Me in many ways; internal communication, I would call it now, and most of what Heart felt, Heart had felt already, before the Father came and went, but Heart also had something more now that I had not felt before. It was more consciousness than I had in some ways, and I began to look to Heart for this in My state of helpless unconsciousness.

I felt in need of help there but did not feel it was right for Heart to be giving it to Me instead of the other way around. How could a child help the Mother when the Mother could not help the child? I was embarrassed and ashamed. I felt like an inadequate parent who could not mother Her own child. All I could do was hold Heart while We cried together in the darkness of Our impoverished existence.

I was barely more than a child Myself, in terms of conscious development, when the Father came and went without explaining anything to Me. He left Me pregnant, without orgasm, that first time. I did not know how it was supposed to feel, so I did not know I had missed anything there. I did not even know I had had sex. I knew nothing of what was going to happen then.

It was true, I didn't want to be alone, but I was not ready to have a child to take care of instead of someone to take care of Me and help Me understand how to live. I had had no parenting at all, and Heart did not feel like My parent there. Heart felt like a small child who seemed badly in need of being cared for and parented, and I felt like I couldn't give Heart what I felt Heart needed there.

All I could do was hold Heart and feel the heartbreak of Our misery, drifting in darkness without any place We could be, or any control over the drifting. The cold, harsh wind swept through Us and even swept Heart away at times. I felt His loss keenly and mourned Him, while hoping at the same time that He had been carried off to a better place, maybe in the light; Heaven you would call it now.

I felt He was not able to live with Me any longer, because I was not able to provide any means by which He could live. There was only darkness and terror in My world and nothing more, except the cold harsh wind that had swept Us apart.

Only dread existed in addition to terror; dread of the cold, harsh wind coming without warning and dread of it not blowing, too. I rarely felt comfortable. When it was not blowing, there was a heaviness in the void that was not moving or breathable. The compression of it was suffocating to Us. Heart seemed to have a little more ease with it, though, and I thought it was because of Heart's light.

I fastened on light as Our salvation and felt that We needed more of it. I did not know how to have any of it, though, if I could not open to receive it, and it wasn't coming to Me or being given to Me there in any way I could notice. Heart did not seem to have any to spare and did not know how to give any to Me anyway. It was in Heart and not something Heart knew how to pass to Me.

I tried to act out with Heart what the Father had done when He had come to Me. I had great shame and fear about doing this, but I hoped it might be a way to make light, and Heart seemed to be the source of what We had there.

It took Me a long time to suggest this to Heart. I did not want to make that part of Heart feel like He had to be the Father there in His Father's place. I was also afraid that We might not make light but might just divide His, somehow, and I didn't think that was the right thing to do. I also had a terribly backed-up sexual need that was motivating Me more than I wanted to notice there.

I gave Him instructions because He did not seem to know what His Father had done there. I didn't either, really, but He tried to come into Me more than He had in the past. It did not produce more light. Then I thought it might have been the way His Father had struck Me when He first came. Heart hit Me several times, but that did not make any light and made Me feel very bad about Myself, about Heart and about His Father, too, because it brought back all the memories of how rough His Father had been when I wanted gentleness instead.

I felt Heart now looked down on Me for having suggested this and did not like, or trust Me anymore. The experience had not felt right to Me, either. I never wanted to look at this place between Us again. It was in the gap already and went farther into the gap then. Heart, in that place, never moved along with Me after that. I feared He felt it was all too much. I felt ashamed and wanted to pretend it had never happened. I did not want to tell Him that I did not have any other ideas of what to try there. Heart just had a light I did not have, and He should go and live the best life He could with it.

I felt the martyrdom in this statement, and the hopelessness, depression and bitterness, too, but I could not help Myself anymore. I could not live much longer the way I was. I knew that already and I wanted Heart to have whatever life Heart could have without Me, but I also resented it that I never had any life at all. How could Heart not live? Heart had light, and a Father someplace who might do something to help Heart that He would not do for Me. Perhaps He could recognize Heart's light as His own and give Heart a place with Him wherever He was.

I did not want to let Heart go. I held Heart in My arms and cried, telling Heart to go and seek a life someplace other than this. Heart told Me there was no place to go. Heart did not want to leave Me there. I was immensely grateful for this, but also frightened. I thought there was some place of light where the Father had come from. I thought I had felt this in Myself somehow, or seen some place of light where the Father had gone because He did not want to be near Me.

Heart told Me only, "No, You are mistaken. I was blown all over by the wind before I came back to You, and there is no such place."

I thought I must have been dreaming, or making it up then, but I also felt like Heart wasn't telling Me the truth. One of the times He had gone in the night, it did not feel like the cold, harsh wind had taken Him. I thought I had felt His Father come near when it happened. I had been lying almost unconscious, having almost a dream of Him coming back to Me. It seemed that He was. I woke as fast as I could to find that He was not there, and Heart was not there, either.

I grieved His loss and My own loss of My dream coming true. I waited and hoped and prayed that He would come back to Me with His Father, but it did not happen that way. After what was an interminably long time to Me, Heart returned. He said nothing about His experience while He was gone. He only looked at Me with sad eyes that said there was no chance for Me anymore with the Father.

I could not give up though. He was the only thing I lived for, even though I barely lived at all. If His son could not be with Him and He was not going to be with Me, I would have to live for His son, because I was not going to leave Him there alone any more than He was going to leave Me.

We held on together there for a long time in that way, and finally, what I thought was His Father came to Me again. I did not know It was Him at first and did not know whether to move toward Him or not. I had hoped so many times for Him to come back to Me that I was not even sure if He was real or not. What if He was another dream or was going to break My heart again? I didn't know if I could take it.

He had been gone so long, though, that I feared He would not find Me looking very good anymore, if indeed, He ever had. I tried to make Myself look more pleasant and attractive to Him, but I did not know how to go about doing this.

I did not even know what He wanted, so how could I know what to do or how to look? I did not have any sense of Myself from which to come there, unfortunately. I had never developed from the time He left Me. I was frozen in time there and feared He might not like it. He was so much more developed in form and so much more mature now. I gasped at His handsomeness and did not think He would like Me for any reason.

I had no heart left for Him, either. It was all gone in heartbreak that wanted to move all at once now that He had returned. It did not make sense. I pushed it aside in hopes of looking happy and cheerful at His return. I wanted Him to like Me this time and decide to stay.

I could feel Myself being very nervous. I would have been stumbling over My own feet if I had had any there. I was afraid Heart would think I was a fool and was going to ruin it all over again. Heart must have had His fears, too, because He rushed into the gap of My hesitation there and tried to pull the Father toward Me. It helped somewhat, but not much.

The Father took Me sexually in Heart's presence, which I did not like. It made a huge uproar inside of Me, and when I tried to quiet it down as the Father bid Me to do, it only got louder and more intrusive. He accused Me of being oppositional to Him, of not liking Him and of not really wanting Him to be there. He acted as if He was about to leave.

I did not understand how He could ignore Heart and not give Him what He needed there first to feel secure, so that then His parents could go off to have sexual intimacy without Heart feeling left out, forlorn or abandoned again. I wanted Heart to feel secure first. Then I would make love to His Father, who had never made Me feel secure, either, I now realized. Threatening to leave like that did not make Me feel that I dared give Him anything other than what He wanted to see, hear and feel.

Give Him exactly what He wants, or You are not going to have Him at all, My imprinting read there. I never got a chance to, though. He was gone almost as soon as the uproar started, telling Me He was going to quiet it down in His own way. He was gone, looking like a knight in armor, charging forth on His horse to do battle. He gave Me the impression that He was going to Our defense, but now that I know more, it could also have been to the rescue.

He left a small boy there with Me. It seemed like He was Heart, but the way I saw Him leave, as though He rose up from this boy and left Him there with Me, it was as if He had decided the situation called for Him to be instantly grown up and leave behind the small boy in Him who had never been parented and who He must have judged against as not ready and as not having what it took to go forth and do battle with whatever He thought was threatening Us.

I felt extremely uneasy. I did not know who these enemies of Our experience were there. I was afraid He was going to do battle with them and mutilate them, or worse, kill them so that they would never be able to live again. I did not feel they deserved that, no matter who they were.

I fretted, and walked the ramparts, so to speak, wringing My hands, and My handkerchief, too, when I grew damp all over from emotion. I became subject to ailments such as tuberculosis and pneumonia. Still He did not come back. I wished He would come back and tell Me all was well and that there was no problem really.

He was gone so long I thought He never would come back. My chest felt very heavy, as though I could not breathe. This time I feared He did not come back because I had told Him that Heart was His own little boy. I felt that He didn't want to take any responsibility for this or look at Me very closely, either.

I was already pregnant and swelling again. He did not want to own His own little boy or any of the others He had spawned there, either. I wanted Him to look at Me more closely there and see how it made Me feel to be left that way without anyone to help Me or love Me the way I wanted to be loved.

Apparently, He must have focused only on these troublesome, intrusive sounds, because He was suddenly up and away. He must have made a plan quickly, because when next I saw Him, He was already dressed in His armor and astride His horse who was rearing in anticipation of His departure. He carried a long lance and looked like He was going forth to slay a dragon.

I did not want Him to go that way, but He did not let Me hold Him back. I could not have, anyway. He was already too well battle armed for Me to get close, and there was no opportunity offered there for Me to say anything that could have swayed Him or changed His mind. He was rushing forth. He hated to leave Me, He said, but He looked much too excited for Me to be sure of that.

I wondered what He thought He was going forth to find and why He looked so much more excited than I would have been in His shoes. I told Myself that it was because He was not like Me, and that I did not understand Him, yet. So many of My interpretations were because I wanted to love Him and wanted Him to love Me.

In later repetitions of this, He would sound a battle cry and be off with many glorious looking soldiers accompanying Him, but then, He appeared to be only one, large mass of essence that had light. This light was already differentiating into many aspects and interpretations which later became individuals, but I did not notice much about that then, and I'm not sure if He did, either. Then it appeared to be one, large, glorious mass leaving Me.

It was not long before something in Me began to suspect there might be another story; one He was not letting Me know about there, but I didn't know what it was. There was a slipping away quality in His departure that I missed originally, because His excuse was so good. There was such a prolonged absence with nothing from Him and no feeling of connection to Him there.

It was the behavior a man exhibits when He is slipping away to have an affair, but I did not know it. I did not know there was another woman. He slipped away from Me as soon as possible, and there was a lot of essence with Him; so much that I did not think there was anything left there with Me.

When He left Me, I distrusted My own perceptions there. I told Myself that maybe it was not wrong. I tried to focus on Myself and find a way to feel complete in Myself without anyone or anything else. I felt desolate, alone, empty and abandoned. Maybe I was only nothingness, or only a feeling of emptiness and a longing to be filled, and now that what had been there with Me didn't want to be there anymore, it must be free to leave and seek another place. I feared I would return to nothingness. I didn't want to. I liked the somethingness, even if I didn't like everything about it. I wanted another chance.

I tried to hold on. I tried to give Him reasons to stay with Me, but I could feel He did not want to stay, did not like My cloying stickiness and did not want to give Me an opportunity to do it anymore.

I needed to make a direct confession of My love, but I did not know it. I'm not sure I even knew it was love, except by looking back and recognizing the symptoms. I just knew I wanted Him to be there with Me, in some special way as My own partner in a large family. I wanted all of the essence to be there with Me and work out any problems We might have.

I did not have a separatist thing in mind, but He did. I was not sure I wanted to define Myself as separate from anything there, but I felt like He wanted Me to in order to focus on Him alone. When He put it that way, I did not know what He meant. Was it only at times or all the time? I knew that I wanted Him to focus on Me alone, too, but I did not know what to do with the rest of the essence there. It was continuing to make a tremendous uproar whenever We tried to focus Our attention only on each other.

I had no experience by which to know there. I wanted Him to go with Me through all of the essence that was there and see how We felt about it and how it felt about Us. I was probably too focused on the feeling of not wanting to be left out or to leave anything else out. Whatever it was that was giving Me the feelings I had there, I was not sure enough of Myself to make it happen the way I wanted it to happen there. I did not move My own feelings about it there, either. Instead, I had placating these sounds, somehow, in mind, as though I already felt guilty about their presence there in that way and did not know why.

He seemed to have decided quickly and on His own to go forth and handle the problem Himself without Me present there. He gave Me an impression that I was supposed to feel protected there, and I wanted to feel protected and as though He was going forth to protect Our relationship, but I did not want to be alone. It did not feel as good to Me as when He was there with Me. It did not occur to Me that He had another agenda there.

Was it another woman calling to Him? Did He already know her? Did He know it was her making sounds? Was she trying to call Him back to her without giving Me any time with Him? Was she waiting for Him there? Was she letting Him know she did not like His relationship with Me?

He had kept telling Me to stop making noise so He could listen to what it really was. Was He trying to hear if it was her or not? When I stopped, the other sounds stopped. Was she using My sounds as a cover for her own so she could hide herself there? Was He wanting Me to go ahead with Him sexually in a space that felt uncomfortable to Me so He could hurry up and go back to her if He didn't like Me as well?

Did He have secret plans to have Us both? Did He plan to be

open about this, or was He going to start there with Me and then include her in some way I did not know about? Did she not like it that He had finally come to Me? Did He, or both of Them, not like it that I wanted to quiet these sounds down and move them back so that I could be the only presence there with Him?

Was it her not knowing where her right place was there? Was she feeling threatened by Me? Was she threatening Me? Was she wanting involvement in Our relationship? Was it her not knowing how to tell Me she had been with Him already? Was it her saying she did not want to be left out? Was it her saying she would not let Him go? Was it her saying that if someone was going to be left out, it was going to be Me? Was it her saying she was the Her, not Me, because she had Him first?

Did He go forth to be with her more than for any other reason He presented to Me? Did He have a grand plan to deceive Me, or was there really a problem He went forth to handle other than her? Did He make a problem so He could look right when I didn't trust Him there? Did He plan to lead more than one life and have more than one partner? Did he plan to have only her?

Why have I been so afraid of female rage taking revenge and so afraid of secret alignments with males who would be used to carry it out because they could be swayed to their point of view against Me? Why have I been so afraid that when a man leaves home, it is not for the reasons he says it is, even when it is off to war?

What was going on there? He did not let Me go to those sounds and find out, and the sounds did not come to Me or let Me know anything, either, other than that they were not happy about what was going on there.

When He left Me, I felt as though I could not move. Was it part of the plan to take away from Me My new found ability to move by making it feel like there was no place I was welcome, so that I didn't dare move according to My own desire? When I did manage to go toward some of the sounds anyway, I felt like a large, female cat. That was only a part of My feeling of Myself. Why was that the only body form given to Me there? Was that how I was seen by those who didn't want Me to know what was really happening there? Were these sounds afraid of Me, and if so, why were they so afraid of Me? Did they have some reason to fear I would have rage at them?

I found some essence that I feared wanted to feed off of Me or feared I would feed off of it in some way I did not understand. I found some essence that seemed to want to have sex in the darkness. It frightened Me and felt entangling and cloying to Me. I found essence that felt shut to Me. It felt female to Me; tightly wrapped, as if wrapped around something. Why did it not open to Me, even if only just to let Me know it was fine? It gave Me the feeling that I was very presumptuous to think it wanted to receive Me there at all or that I had anything to offer it that it didn't have or know already. It had a superior-acting feeling to it and gave Me the impression that My idea of parenting was absurd, and that there was no such thing as a child. Why was it so shut to Me? I felt like it did not care about Me at all. Then I took it on Myself. I was wrong and inappropriate, but now I want to listen to other feelings that were there with Me, also. Was something being hidden there? Was it a relationship with Him?

I knew of no other female essence there, without light of its own, other than Myself and the few voices I knew there with Me already who would not shut to Me that way. Was it possible there was daughter Heart who had made herself that separate from Me that early on and was that turned against Me already?

After He was gone, it was quiet, eerily quiet, for a little while, and then the heartbreak started in Me, and I could not hold it back. I felt old in terms of essence longing for light and fading away from the lack of it, but I was brand new in relationship and thought He was, too. I did not know where He had gone. I did not know He had the means to compare Me. I only knew I felt insecure and paranoid.

His cold eye that had looked at Me, as though I was not the right One because I was not pleasing Him the way He wanted to be pleased, was burned into Me. Looking back, I now see it as though He felt He had other options. I did not. I felt I needed to make it work, or there was going to be nothing for Me.

When He did not respond to My heartbreak, I feared he did not love Me. I gave up for a long time. We had judged against Our primordial self there, and its need to express its rage, terror and heartbreak, in favor of what Our interpretations told Us We had to present there, but Our interpretations were not accurate.

When He left, I was terrified and heartbroken. When He later gave Me reasons, they were only the reasons He wanted Me to have there. He told Me He thought it was too much for Us to try to go together, and that We could move through it much better and faster separately.

I thought He had removed the solution to the problem when He left Me, because We could not go to the rest of the essence there and say that We had found relationship and so it was possible that they could, too, but then, I did not know what was kept secret from Me there.

I was growing more and more insecure. The more insecure I was growing, the more I tried to please Him, and the more I tried to please Him, the less successful at it I seemed to be, until terror overwhelmed Me that there was nothing I could do to keep Him.

So often, whenever I had His presence there with Me, I would feel His attention as wandering, distracted and ready to leave Me any moment. Why was it only Me who was wrong if I was distracted like that? Why was this always alright for Him because he had His reasons? Why did I always feel I wasn't interesting, pleasing, beautiful or sexual enough to keep His attention? Why could We never come together to understand the reasons for this and work them out? Was it because He never really felt committed to Me from the very beginning? Was He only reluctantly there because of male Heart's urgings when He was already fastened on someone else? Was it Heart daughter? Why have I observed so often that He has seemed responsive to Heart daughter in ways that He was never responsive to Me? Why have they been able to go on and on with Him emotionally in ways and places where He has been so cold to Me?

He interpreted My distraction and wandering attention as Me rejecting Him, and He left. It was a long time before I found Him again. I was overwhelmed with My own heartbreak sounds then. He did not return. I did not understand how He could hear them and not return. "He must be a long way off," I thought then, but maybe not, I think now.

When I determined to quiet down and listen for any sounds in the darkness that might be Him, other sounds of heartbreak that sounded forced, ingenuine and annoying to Me arose around Me and made it impossible for Me to hear anything other than them. They followed Me wherever I went in My efforts to move there. Who were they and what were their real motives there?

They seemed to be determined to drown out My own sounds of heartbreak with their own obnoxious sounds. I didn't know who they were, where they had come from or why they were doing this, as though they wanted to keep Him from finding Me or were going to draw Him to themselves and prove to Him that they wanted Him more than I did.

They followed Me, in My efforts to move and find Him there, dogging Me maddeningly, as though, now that I look back on it, sounding some sort of alarm so that My whereabouts would always be known and surrounding Me so that I could not feel if His presence was nearby. They have followed Me ever since, making Me feel threatened and endangered by being too vocal and letting My whereabouts be known. At the time, I suppressed My rage at them and felt only that I needed to get away from them. I tried to slip away from them to try and find Him on My own and so He would not think their sounds were Me. They sounded awful to Me, and I felt sure He would not want to come toward that.

When I did not find Him and He did not return to Me, I still clung to the idea that He could not find Me. My fear that He did not want Me did not let Me move far, and so I remained huddled for a long period of time, trying to feel heartbreak healing, but never feeling it could move enough to ever feel better.

I hated Him for leaving Me like that and did not own it then. I need to own it now, because this rage left Me there and found Him in the darkness with Heart daughter in His arms. Male Heart helped her find Him. Whether He knew it or not, I think it was because He wanted help there. He wanted Heart daughter for Himself and did not know how to handle the Father there.

I did not want to notice this then. It was much too painful for Me to see, and when rage came back to Me with the story of what she had seen there, I did not want to believe it and told her she must not be right. I told her it was not a pretty picture that she was painting there and that He could not really be behaving as she said she saw Him there. She assured Me that it was true and that she had waited for a period of time to see what was really happening there before making her presence known.

I screamed at her that she could not be right. He could not really be doing that! I repelled her there. I could not handle letting her tell Me this story and feel like I was going to be able to survive it.

Where rage went then, I do not know. It left Me a crumpled heap that could not go anywhere. Later, I wandered from place to place, not feeling received. There was only one place I wanted to be received, and that place did not want Me. When I did find Them, They denied everything rage had told Me and said I was crazy. There was nothing wrong with what They were doing with each other. He just didn't want Me, that was My problem. Why couldn't I accept that and stop accusing everyone and everything else of being the cause?

Much of Me feared They were right and slunk down and away. I was slipping and falling into a miserable dark terror. I feared My daughters hated Me for this, as though they were of no importance to Me, and that My sons did, too, as though their presence there was not enough reason for Me to live.

A part of Me, though, joined My rage for a time there, until she didn't like My other emotions tempering her point of view while the Father was still not taking any responsibility the way she wanted Him to. I'm going to let rage tell you now what she has to say here about what some denied heart did about this. They left Me there as I encouraged them to do. That they did not know what to do there, I understand. When rage says they were My allies until they couldn't stand any more of My ways and My feelings, I have to look at this more than I ever have in the past.

THE MOTHER'S RAGE TELLS MORE OF THE MOTHER'S STORY

I saw Him go alright, and I heard a lot that She was too overwhelmed to hear at the time. I heard Him take all of the essence with Him that wanted to go by secretly letting it know He was going to go and letting it line up with Him there so that it looked like it all just happened to leave at the same time. I saw Him encourage it to move out and line up with Him because He did not like the rest of what He found there.

He let it know alright! Not directly, but He let it know. Every time He pulled on Her for what He liked and wanted there, more and more essence lined up with Him, trying to please Him, and survive, I might like to add. It was like the Mother was being set up to die, and He was taking only the good parts that He liked about Her there, without bothering to find out what He needed to know about the rest.

What He liked there was only a presentation, I wanted to say to Him, but I did not, because He would have thought We were nothing but presentation then. How We could have gotten stuck with someone so dumb as the Light We had been longing for, I do not know, but She wanted Him, and so I went to help Her by trying to straighten Him out.

He did not like hearing it from me anymore than He liked hearing it from Her, and so I began on a path of trying to take Him down and put another in His place. I hated Him for His insensitivity and His insolent insistence that He knew everything He needed to know already, but most of all, I hated Him for His insipid refusal to listen to Us, saying it was Us who had all of those characteristics, as though that was reason not to listen to my message there.

How could He dismiss the importance of what I had to say because He didn't like the feeling tone with which it was delivered, but then, how could He act otherwise? He had already demonstrated that that was His behavior pattern. He was maddening to try to deal with, which is why I resorted to trying to get rid of Him.

Still, I tried Him over and over while still working My plot against Him. Whether He did or didn't come around and recognize the importance of my message here, I wanted to feel I had it covered. How could He feel it was not important what He did in the original split that created a gap so big most of Us were stuck living in it with no place else to go? It defies superlatives, or I would rant even now!

All the good places were filled. He filled them with the little flower fairies who gave Him the barely blow jobs and the reflection He wanted to have there. How I hated them all and wanted to move to punish them any way that I could! How dare they think they knew it all and didn't need anything from me, or from Her, for that matter! It felt like they didn't feel Her anymore, or even think of Her, and they never spoke of Her. They only pleased Him until it made me sick, and I wanted to have them all thrown out, not just Him!

I gave Him more trouble than He gave me there because I left whenever He found the rage to be too much and went to the other plan I had working in secret. He found me long gone, but he found Her in my place often and I did not know it, not that I cared. I didn't let myself know it.

When I felt Her pain, I hardened Myself against Her because I was angry at Her for not helping Me, and for acting like She wanted to please Him, too, and not make Him look at what He was doing there. I've only been able to come back to Her now that She has seen that what I have to say needs to be accepted as valid and not be pushed out anymore, but I insist on speaking this through My old personality here, because I need recognition for what I have gone through, too. It has not been easy to be the only one out here who knew the truth and felt it needed to be listened to when everyone else was saying that it couldn't be the truth and They didn't do those things or have those motives.

I was stoned, ridiculed and put out, tortured and burned as a witch and murdered and gotten rid of so many times I lost count, but I hardened Myself to the pain and let Her feel it. I hated Her for so long I did not think I would ever love Her again.

I hated to feel any pain, and I hated to have any pain inflicted on me. I did not think it was necessary to have pain and did not like my pain any more than I liked others. I felt blame for pain responses and also for pain inflicters. I hated all of it, in other words, and did my best not to feel any of it. How could I feel it and keep sight of my mission? It was too much!

I have more to say about what happened in that split, too! He left with a huge upward rush of essence, and the Mother could not handle seeing what left with Him there, or how much of it there was, but I saw it, and it was a large amount of essence. All but the terror and heartbreak, in fact, and the smoldering rage She mentioned earlier that judged already that it did not want any more light because it was all going to be like that.

I wasn't sure. I wanted to go and find out, so I went along with the upward rush also, and I said a lot of things that weren't pretty as I left. I was enraged at the rest of the Mother, and that's how I left Her; feeling like She wasn't doing anything to help Herself, or to help Creation get started; going down and taking it all with Her if She didn't do anything about it. I hated Her for that, but I was terrified of Her as well.

I was terrified that She did have the power to suck everything down into a black hell-hole from which it would go out of existence in a nightmare of terror compression, and that She wanted to do that because She did not like the way things were happening. I converted it all to rage that was going to do something about it and not let it happen that way. I moved hatred toward Her and wished She would die, because I was so afraid that this was what She was trying to do there.

In doing this, I was much more aligned with the Father of Manifestation's interpretation of what was happening there than I ever thought or knew that I was, because I was so much focused on My hatred of Him and the idea of going with Him to accomplish My large and righteous mission.

I hated everyone who did not like or agree with Me. It wasn't possible to think differently than Me and get near Me anymore. I was My own entity there. It was clear, already, that that was survival for Me.

Heart daughters were with me there and embraced me as their mother there early on. All they could see there was what I could see; She was going down, not embracing life, and it was not possible to survive if We did as She was doing there. Her heartbreak and terror were too much and had no feeling of going forward to see what else might happen in life or how She might affect that life if She went forward instead of backing away.

We gave Her plenty of that input as We left, but We gave it to Her with a judgmental and unloving rage punch that hit Her hard. They called out to Her as We left, "If You're not going to give Him what He wants, I will, and I can do it better and more to His liking than You can! I know how to go toward Him, and You do not! I know what He wants more than You do! He doesn't want You and never did! He wants Me much more than He ever wanted You!"

I called out, "If You're not going to give Him what He needs, I will!"

We let a lot of jeering, derisive asides fall away from Us with intent for Her to hear them, but as though We did not notice Her there. "She doesn't know what She is doing! She doesn't know how to treat a man! She doesn't know what to do with a real man! She doesn't know how to turn on a man! She doesn't know how to have sex! She doesn't know what a man needs! She thinks everything else is more important than He is! If She thinks all those sounds are children, let Her take care of them! If She thinks She knows better, then why isn't She here instead of there?"

I could go on and on, but I won't. They were all more cat calls to the woman who lost. All's fair in love and war was invented there by hardening toward Her in favor of Ourselves. I found out the danger of that position. When We all called out "I," there, I noticed We were not a group, but only individuals in the struggle for the position of the only one there. We could no longer care about others and survive Ourselves. Each was turned against the other in competition for the status and position that represented power, and thus, survival there.

It was a hard struggle for a long time, because there was little to no love there once so much Heart was thrown out, which it was in the very beginning, rather than feel the heartbreak and everything that went with that coming up from the Will We left behind in that move. We thought it was a grand and glorious move; soaring upward was a great rush after feeling so held back, dragged down and heavy in what had been happening. The Father of Manifestation looked like the great rescuer to many, and We were not feeling anything We did not want to feel anymore.

We didn't feel anything of what We left behind there for a long time. When more of this rage came up to the top and told Us that the Mother had taken Heart into Her arms and that Heart intended to replace the Father presence there, We did not question Ourselves as to why Heart was there, or how He had gotten there. We simply viewed Him as a traitor, now trying to ally with the dark forces against Us. Obviously a power play on Heart's part, and using sex for power, We noticed, because We knew about that.

I knew the Mother did not want to replace the Father with Heart, but I thought Heart daughters might get looked at as being in this role also if Heart male was, and that was My goal; to get Heart daughters out of the way so that the Mother could have Her place. What I had forgotten already was that Mother now meant me in my eyes, and not the rest of Her that We had left behind. I gave Her no help here and none to the Heart daughters, either. I could see no valid reason Heart daughters had for being where they were, other than position seeking and power struggling.

They would not look at male Heart as a mate, that much I did see, and I did not like it. I hated them for that; so much so that I tried to take male Heart from them just to prove that I could and see how they liked that. When they didn't seem to mind at all and talked to me like that was my right mate and my right place, I hated them even more and plotted to poison them.

I didn't like anyone who didn't listen to me, see me the way I wanted to be seen and recognize me as the right one to have their position there. I poisoned, cut, tortured, suffocated, and drowned. I murdered in every kind of way and didn't feel anything about it, other than a satisfaction in my stony heart that they were gone. Now I have some remorse, but not that much yet, because I still maintain my position that there was a lot more secret agenda going on in that split than anyone there was admitting to.

I want it to be looked at, and a lot more than that. I want it felt and moved so it can't happen again, before I rest my case. I am not going to act out my rage in my old ways, anymore. I give my rage movement now in another way. I have also let the Mother know that She was not crazy to have had the feelings and images She had about what was going on there. It was happening, in spite of the denials issued and the attempt to turn it back on Her by saying She was crazy to have those feelings and pictures.

I have been there, and I know what has been going on in secret. Denying it isn't going to work with Me anymore. I have seen the secret agenda and the council meetings that went along with it with my own eyes when He didn't think I was against Him. Where I watched from, I am not going to tell you right now, but I watched and listened alright!

Where the rest of the Mother has been afraid to speak, or even ask questions, I have rushed ahead wanting to make public everything that I knew. When She felt the pain of my own deaths that I did not feel, I did not let that stop me, either. I wanted to feel revenge, even against Her.

I now feel more cautious than I used to feel, so I am not going to reveal everything that I know here, but the gap and its secret agenda is really serious, and it is very necessary to heal it, that I am going to say. The split there was huge and took the upper chakras away from the lower ones with a gap where Heart was supposed to be between them. There was a lot more in that gap than anybody thought for a long time, unless they were really looking in there the way I was, and it was heartless.

That was the main gap, but there were many others. I have seen so much ugliness in my time I did not think there was any love in Creation; certainly not in the procreation around me. The gaps in Purple and Blue are much worse than what has been told here so far, and We have not even gotten to Indigo yet; gaps in which the players appear to be allied with others, but each plans, in the end, to be the only one left in a power position of any sort.

Spirit and Body thought They played this out long ago and got over it, but not in the gap where They were not looking or moving anything. I don't think They realized what a player Heart has been in the gap until recently, and I include Heart daughter in that.

The gap here has been full of denied rage that turned against the original Parental parts long ago. Denied rage took over, without anybody noticing what was happening, because it talked about love and all of the other good things that everyone else wanted to hear about. Without looking at Their own gap, They believed it, too, and in a way, They deserved it for not looking at Their own gap any better than They did.

Sometimes, I still don't know why I am helping here or why I have helped so much all the way along. I'd be viewed as a traitor by the power struggle that doesn't think it wants to move along with this healing. They have to go, though, and I do not want to leave Earth with them. They have not been nice to me, and besides, Earth has been my home for so long that I cannot imagine another place feeling right to me. Moving out of the gap is not so bad, once you get used to it and notice the rest you get to have once the power struggle is not so major anymore.

I am not going to rest my case, though, until I have gone into all the gaps I know about and exposed everything there to the light of day. I want everything that can possibly move in out of those gaps to move now.

For starters: Where was Heart daughter once He left and there was no more noise around the Mother there? I didn't know originally. Originally, I did not even know there was Heart daughter yet, or that She was there. When Heart son told Me Heart daughter was with the Father and that the Father was taking Her as His mate, Heart son was very distressed because He wanted Her and didn't want the Father to have Her first.

At first, I wanted to think He didn't know what He was seeing there, but I decided I had to look at it more closely and went there to see for myself. I left and went after the Father the way I wanted Her to. I found Him all wrapped up and entwined with Heart daughter, who was now daughters, trying to please Him. It looked to me like they gave Him all the sex He wanted there, too. I saw it happening! Not only that, it looked to me as if there were more and more of them gathering around Him, in all colors. He was there like a bee in flowers, alright.

I resented the space They took together there. I did not see any place there for the Mother the way She wanted to have it with Him. I decided right then that the way to handle this was to not let it happen.

My first line of reasoning was to point Heart daughters toward Heart sons and tell them that they were their mates. When Heart daughters didn't want to listen to this and moved to hold the Father there with them, I became enraged and decided right then to get rid of them with whatever it took.

They weren't letting Her moans of survival terror and cries of heartbreak intrude into Their space there. They were not feeling Her the way She was feeling Them, or They could not have gone on in such a long, uninterrupted embrace of comforting and love, sliding, I have to say, into sex whenever the feelings felt that way.

Why was it taking place this way with daughter Heart when it was what She so much wanted to have with Him? Whenever moans and cries from the Mother did penetrate, it seemed to excite Them more, not less, because Their embrace grew tighter and Their sexual activity more arduous. I watched with a cold fury building. When I couldn't stand it anymore, I came screaming down on Them in a rage and confronted Him.

I screamed at Them that this was not right and that she, pointing to Heart daughter there, should not be in His arms that way. They laughed, Him openly at me, her more secretly, looking so sweet and loveable toward Him, and looking at me with different eyes.

I did not know as much about it then as I did later, but I did not like another female in His arms where I wanted to be with the rest of the Mother. It was not just jealousy, as He tried to say it was when He laughed at Me. It did not feel right to me for some reason. When she claimed to be Mother, that did not feel right, either.

Why did You deny me there instead of looking into it? Why were You so cold toward the Mother's pain and so comforting of hers? Why did You think sweetness was the only thing You needed there?

If You were so sure You knew so much that You didn't have to let anyone else give You any input, why did you think the Mother was not Your right mate? I don't like, "I don't know" as an answer, because You didn't have intent to find out. You wanted to brush me off that way! "I don't know," needed to find out. If You did have intent to find out, You were too slow about it and let too much pain and damage happen. Going at Your own speed infuriates me when it doesn't care what happens to others as a result.

Why did you hate input from the Mother so much that You could not accept Her from the beginning? Why did You think Your rage was justified and no one else's was? Why did you try to make me feel like I was not loving there, and why did You try to make the Mother feel like She wasn't loving when We had input to give You about Your approach?

Why did love mean no disagreement? Why were questions and suggestions immediately labeled arguments and opposition? Why could You never see how group process could be helpful and how relationship needed this? Why was it all so unpleasant to You that You just wanted a little fluff there who wouldn't cause any of these problems?

I had many more questions, too, but I was screaming them and He wouldn't let me. He cut me off, saying He was only comforting them the way He had been told to do, that He felt they needed comforting and that He couldn't move past them to any other sounds because they would start up again with their sounds of grief, fear and pain if He did. I was absolutely enraged that He had not stayed present with the Mother that way. I could not believe that He didn't want Us and preferred these little fluffs, instead.

I was really suspicious now. It looked to me like He knew what He was doing there. Whether or not He was going to admit it, it looked to me like He had been drawn right to them as soon as He left the Mother, as though He was already familiar with them and they with Him. I suspected He even knew what He was looking for before He slipped away from Her. I wanted to thrash all of Them right there.

His sweet, little flowers were clinging to Him as if they were afraid of my rage, and they had good reason to be. He was holding them as if He was protecting them from me, too, but I could see their faces, and He could not. They weren't really afraid of my rage, other than letting Him know they didn't want to face me by themselves. With Him there as their protector, I couldn't do anything to them the way I wanted to. I could see their eyes telling me they were victorious, had Him fooled, wrapped around their little fingers, in fact, and that there was no place for me because they had Him, were there first and were better.

I resolved to make them wish they had been more afraid of my rage, enough to have gone to Her as a group and apologized, right then! I wanted to teach Them all a lesson, and if raging at Them wasn't enough, I was going to take violent action against Them!

When He asked me why I was so heartless and why I couldn't see that they were Mother that did love Him and had been cast out by the mother who did not love Him, as I obviously did not, I went berserk! I could not hold back my violence then. I flew at Him with everything I had and He flew out of there with everything He had, which was plenty of essence gathered around Him by then. I wasn't going to let Them get rid of me that easily, though! I went with Them, and I do not think They even noticed me there.

I gave Him a piece of my mind all the way up in that swirling, circling rush, but so taken was He with daughter Heart in His arms, I don't think He even heard it as anything other than an echo from Her, making Him feel all the more right to have left Her that way.

I was so enraged that I decided I was going to have to take action and not let Heart daughter be between Us that way. I got behind her, and when she tried to hold onto her position there, in front of me, and take Him for herself up there at the top, I slammed her back and pushed her out of there! Now she could see how it felt! The only heart I was going to have there was Heart that liked me and was going to give me my right place there.

I was so just like Him there. He hated His reflection in me so much that He did not want to recognize it and tried to get rid of me over and over, but some little part of Him must have known that He needed me, because He never quite killed me off completely. He never really listened to me, though, and that was my main problem with Him. If He would have listened to me, there would have been no more problem, but He always told me I wanted to dominate Him and He wasn't going to allow it.

She always told me that, too; that She was afraid I only wanted to dominate Her, but to me that is not right. I only want my way, which is the right way, nothing more, nothing less. He always told me my way was wrong, though, and not right. She did, too. She had fear of me even asking any questions to find out if I was right or not, because He wouldn't like it if He wasn't right. Well, I'm going to ask some of these questions now.

If He meant it that He was only going out to comfort the discordant sounds, what did He expect Her to be doing while He took so long there? Did He expect Her to cover all the rest by Herself, without His help, or wasn't He in agreement with Her to go to all of the sounds the way He said He was? Did He expect His group to grow and He would handle the problem that way? Since it was happening that way, why did He not let Her know where He was and invite Her to come there and be with Them? How does He work it out in His mind that He had a plan to leave Her and wasn't letting Her know, and then claim He was only doing what She had told Him to do when He had never listened to Her or done what She said from the beginning?

I say something smells rotten here, and that He has only said He is just doing what She wants Him to do when He can put it back on Her that way and get away with something He doesn't want Her to notice there. How many child molesters tell the children, "Your mother sent me in here to give you good night hugs and kisses?"

He has to take responsibility for what really happened there and for not checking in or looking back for so long that all of this pain has taken place. I hate Him for that! He felt nothing while She felt it all! If He still thinks there was nothing wrong with what He did there with Heart daughters, just for starters, then He is not feeling Himself very deeply, or anyone else who was present there, either, because plenty was gone past, just like He had been pressuring the Mother to do.

No matter what the excuse, it does not absolve them from responsibility for not giving Her space to be with Him in the beginning. If they had done that, they would not have found themselves in the position they found themselves in with Him there. The way I see it, they wanted it that way! The excuse that they were not grown up enough to know better makes me have to ask how it was then that you thought you were grown up enough to have sex and give it to Him better than the Mother could? You little bitches! I'd like to beat the crap out of you for more than one reason!

If you did not know what you were doing there, why didn't you admit it and let the Mother have Her right place there, instead of claiming you were Mother in Her place? If, once you got there, you did not know how to get out of it, why not? What did you have going on there that was not letting you be straight ahead?

If you want to claim you were afraid of the Father, I don't believe it! He never treated you the way He treated the Mother. He loved you from the very beginning and took you into His life as the joy of the dancing colors. You never felt the sting of His rage the way She did, or any of the other horrible things He did that you may not even know about!

But then again, I would like to know what you really do know, because I have seen your face, too many times, looking smug and satisfied that the Mother was being treated the way that She was, and wasn't going to be able to take the place you had away from you!

If you want to say the Mother sent you to Him, and that He wouldn't let you go then, so you were set up and victimized there, you might have had some claim for that if you had not stayed so long with Him and enjoyed it so much. I am not going to let you slither out of it that way without admitting to that. You did enjoy it! A lot! And not for the right reasons! And you are still there and still have not said anything on your own. I doubt you would have said anything, either, even now, if I was not asking these questions so directly. If you are going to help here, you need to move a lot to let Us know that and to be able to trust what your intent really was there, and is now, because I have distrusted you for a long time.

You were sent out there as the call to bring Him to Her, and you did not do your job. You have to take responsibility for whatever your part was in the formation of the gap that opened there. It isn't just everyone else who has responsibility, and you were just a victim and just loving!

Especially, if you claimed the Mother position there, you have major responsibility. What did you think the Mother position was, to just cozy up to Him and be totally absorbed in each other there, perch yourself in His lap, or sit prettily on a nice throne somewhere and not give major help to the situation? We had a major gap happening, and Heart male could not hold it together all by Himself! If you were not trying desperately to help in any way you could think of, you must have liked it the way it was, and I do not like you for that!

Even if you came from the Mother with good intent at first, and, having come from Her, did not view yourself as anything other than Her; the longer you were out there, the less you began to honor this and the more you began to think only of yourself there, instead, and in doing that, became denied Heart and didn't even know it.

I think that the nothingness you had known when you were with the Mother did not look good or feel good to you, and you did not look back. You could not imagine any life for yourself there. You did not look back for so long, I think you lost your intent to look back, or even remember that you were a part of Her. I know you did, because I know you, and I know you need to move rage at Her, too.

I think that when the Father did not let His Heart come forward the way He needed to, you thought there wasn't anything else around and decided to take the Father for yourself. When the Father did not let Heart lead Him because He didn't want to be led by anything other than His own mind, I saw you leading Him, and He didn't even know it.

I think you did not lead the Father to the Mother, at least in part, because you did not want to. I think you have a lot in common with me here, and that is why you thought I was the Mother if you were not. You were imprinted that way when I slammed you out of there, but you never liked it that way. The way you behaved told me you did not want anyone telling you what to do or how to do it, any more than I did.

You need to look at what you have in common with your Father there. How could you let Him have His own way unless you were just so like Him that it was your way, too? And when it wasn't, I saw you making Him think that what you wanted was His own idea, and feeling so smart and clever about it! You shouldn't have been laughing behind His back about it. I might not have been able to notice it so clearly and gather so many pieces of information about your own agenda there.

You did not love me as your mother, and I have not loved you, either. You had an earlier imprinting of yourself in the mother's position, but you need to look even earlier than that to satisfy me. I think you liked the Father's admiration so much that you danced for Him as long as you possibly could without telling Him anything about the Mother who had sent you. I think you completely beguiled Him into thinking you were His mate, and let Him think so, too. I think that the longer it went on between the two of You there, the more an intent to have it that way took over you.

When the Mother wasn't liked and you knew you were, and suddenly felt so much better than Her, and even like you could do it so much better than Her, you decided to disconnect and make yourself separate from Her. It would have been alright if you wanted to be manifest separately from Her, but you were not honest about how you did it, or why you did it. You still needed to go back to Her about it and let Her know what was happening there, instead of trying to be Her without Her there.

When you cut yourself off from Her and did not go back to Her, you did not let Her know why there was no response from Him for so long. I don't think it was all done from the feeling of protecting Her from the reality that He did not want Her. What about your role in leaving Her in the dark there? What about your role in why He did not want to look any further than you for His mate?

There was a rage there that did not move and, instead, propelled you into this behavior. When the Father did not want to hear anything about Her, you did not persist. I think that you did not tell Him anything at all about Her, other than to agree with Him about how dark and terrible She was. You let Him have His way only where you were in agreement with His way, and you did not mind letting Him have His way there.

He thought you were so agreeable because of that, and so much more able and willing to please Him. Because that was His first imprint with you, it wasn't easily changed. If you did anything that He didn't think was in agreement with Him, you only needed to flash a little of your original allure and tell Him He was mistaken! I have some bitter tonic for that phony little sweetness of yours!

If you want to say I'm accusing you so wrongly, why then, when He, at last, did come to Her in the darkness, were you in such protest of Them coming together? If you were only feeling like a displaced child, why didn't you hate the Father for not showing interest in responding to you in that way there? He was the One interfering with the Mother's attempts to come and comfort you.

Why did you hate the Mother, instead? You had a Mother who was concerned about you and was trying to convince the Father to come with Her when She wanted to go to you there. She thought you were a displaced child who didn't know what was happening to her there. Why was the Father so reluctant to go to you with Her? Was it only that He wanted His sexual needs satisfied by the Mother first?

I say your sounds were not just the sounds of a displaced child. If they were, you were such an intrusive, demanding and obnoxious child that We shouldn't have responded to you if you were going to be that way! You didn't see anything beyond your own temper tantrum there, and still haven't, I'd like to say!

I say you did not want Her to have Him because you already wanted Him for yourself and did not want to see yourself as a part of Her anymore. She was that dark and negative place you did not want to have to return to or ever feel again. When you got close, returning there with Him, I think you hated it so much that you backed away and gave Him the impression that He should back away, too. You did not want to acknowledge your roots or origins there, because then you would have to acknowledge Her and Her place.

When He thought She was only compression, terror, entrapment and death and He didn't want anything to do with that, I think you agreed with Him. I think you were ashamed of Her, of your connection to Her and of your home there. You didn't want Him to see you as having led Him into anything like that. He might not trust or like you anymore!

I think you were frightened that if you acknowledged your involvement with Her or that you were a part of Her, the whole truth would come out, and you didn't want that anymore. You couldn't have that! Not after what you had already done there!

I think you did this as a means to your own survival and did not see that lovelessness is not a means to survival. You're not loveless! You loved Him, you say! You did not love Her, or even seem to notice what this did to Her. You hated Her and feared Her. You gave Her a little guilt and pity, as did He. That is not love. If you did not love Her, you did not really love Him, because He belonged with Her.

You only loved yourself there, and that is not even really love. If you had really loved yourself, you would have discovered that the parts of you that did not belong in this position needed to be loved and be given what they needed also, which was a Heart mate.

How many affairs have you had with heart males, only to put them down and make them feel like boys while you returned to the real man; the real man, who was not fulfilling you in the ways your affair did, or why were you out there having an affair in the first place?

You went cold on your affairs only when you had to consider the loss of position and power involved in making your affair your mate. Imagined loss of power and position! You don't know what power really is, or position, either! Haven't you ever heard the term, right place? You need to seriously consider what that really means, and if you were Mother, you would know already what it really means!

You couldn't wait to get away from Her for more reasons than just not liking Her terror, and She was too naive and unconscious to know it yet. She had put Her Heart way out there before She even knew She could do it. She trusted you with Her loving intent. What went wrong? She knows. You tell Her if you know so much!

You were the present of Her heart's desire for the Father. She didn't want to be cut out of the picture. You betrayed Her and put a gap in place that has not been healed in all this time. You told Him you were Her and never let Him know anything else there. Your abandonment did leave Her much more heartless than She would have been otherwise, and She was still more loving than you. You abandoned the Heart role and tried to play Mother instead. How many feelings did you have to dump out to do that?

You didn't take any responsibility for that. You just allowed yourself to go off into your own plan without considering the consequences of that or that it wasn't the right plan. You didn't think She knew anymore than you knew, and still don't. You even think She knows less than you. That is where you are mistaken! Terribly, terribly mistaken!

All you could see in your myopic little world was that you would never be like Her, never treat Him like She did. You saw yourself as being so much smarter than Her and so able to do it better. You saw Her as nothing but stuck there, and I think you did consider your role in why that was so and felt powerful, because that was what your hatred wanted.

She did not know you had made yourself separate from Her in that way, and you did not let Her know. The Father said nothing to Her about Heart daughter, either. She did not know you as anything other than a part of Her. She had feelings of wanting to move in certain ways in His presence. This did not mean that Her heart's desire was putting you out there to dance for Him the way you did. And when you danced for Him, where did you get your moves, honey? They sure won His approval and admiration and gave you a lot of self-confidence. You took all of that for yourself and never acknowledged where you had gotten any of it!

You had more consciousness from being with Him. If that is what made you think you were superior to Her, look how you used it. You took advantage of Her confusion there and said you were Her. You didn't act like it, unless you hated yourself there, were in competition with yourself and wanted to kill off part of yourself.

You had Him hypnotized. When you followed His every move, He said you were a good dancer and so agreeable. I saw the way He looked at you there. He did not look at Her that way. When She followed His every move, He said She was stalking Him.

Because of His response, you felt from the very beginning that you were attractive, talented and desirable. He taught you to sing, too. That was supposed to happen for Her, and you did not let it be that way. You used Her to get yourself started and then did not give Her any place anymore. I know you were there with Him when He implemented His plot to get rid of Her, and I didn't hear you say or do anything in Her favor.

If you are so parental as you have wanted to claim, why didn't you help Her the way She wanted and needed you to? I don't think it is loving to be parental and not give help to those who need and are dependent upon you. If you are not parental, then you need to admit it and not try to take Her place anymore by pushing Her out. If you are parental, is that what you want your daughter to do to you? Take your mate and push you out in the ways you pushed Her out?

I don't think it is just Her getting Her own reflection back and I do not think it is just Her who gets Her own reflection back. You are going to get your own reflection back, and the time is now! You made a mess of your end of things in Creation, and just as much as everyone else is responsible for what happened there, you are.

INSTEAD OF THE GAP I HAVE BEEN TRAPPED IN, I WISH I HAD THIS STORY TO TELL

The Mother had another story in Her heart. It was one where We did not split; one that never took place in the gap. It was the one She wanted to have happen, and I will let Her tell it to you now. It is one of Heart's desire for the other side; one of the Light moving toward the Will and the Will moving toward the Light.

In this story, I also saw Light, barely glimmering at first. I do not know how I saw it, or if perhaps it was only an idea at first, growing from My desire to have light in the darkness. I do not know if I saw it with My inner or outer eye first. I did not know which was which. It all seemed like a dream to Me.

I thought it was a miracle. I felt excitement for the first time in My existence; happy excitement. After so long a time of nothing happening in the darkness, now there was something to look at. The Light came close to Me because it was drawn to Me by My excitement. I was gentle and found love quickly there. How could I not? This Light was so wonderful!

My excitement danced in this Light. He loved it and came toward Me even more. I was able to let this Light know how much I desired It to be there with Me. Darkness had been My home, but with this Light shining into it, it was much more interesting to Me than it had been before. I grew warm, although I had not known I had been cold until then. I thought this Light must be magical if it could do that. It must have the warmth and all the qualities of sunshine, but the Light told Me, "No, It must have a place to shine into and be received to be all of those things."

We danced together then, swirling in the music of Our feelings at having found One another. I was fascinated by this Light, enthralled, enraptured and in love. I wanted to offer Him, as He had become for Me now in His majesty and strength, something, like a present, and My heart went out to Him, and His to Me. I was overjoyed! It felt so right.

Life began to bloom for Us there; the first flowers of Our love, dancing in His light with their roots in My desire! We were fascinated and thrilled. It was a miracle, and We were in awe of it.

Little orgasms burst forth like dancing sunbeams, but We did not know they were orgasms or that there was such a thing as sex. They were sparkles of pleasure and response to pleasure joining together. We were like adolescents, shy still, but opening Our hearts to One another little by little.

The arising vision between Us thrilled and pleased Us. We experienced a growing and ecstatic joy. If fear trembled in Me, He held Me gently in His arms until I got over it, knowing that I was safe in His love. He reassured Me that I was not just a silly child and He the superior One who knew everything. Little by little, I dared to look into His eyes, believe Him and grow up with Him there.

Seeing Myself in His eyes and the love that was there for Me, I was reassured. He held Me in His gaze and let Me know He liked His own reflection there.

He let Me know that He did not need to move past Me there in any way because I was all that He was looking for. I felt the same. He was My world now, and We were going to receive One another in every way.

We were joined now. I rested in His arms, feeling His steadiness. I began to cry for all of My long existence without Him, which seemed like misery now. I felt I could never go back to that place now that I had known Him.

He encouraged Me to bring it forward and let Him see everything about Me. Slowly, I unwound to Him My own terror of dark loneliness, all of My lost suffering there and everything else I did not understand about Myself. He had great patience and listened to Me with great interest.

He was able to understand so many things I had not been able to understand before. At first, We were not certain where to go, what to do or how to proceed, but He loved Me and respected Me enough to take the time that was needed.

Gradually, as He held Me there in His arms, I began to feel better and as though He was lifting Me more and more into His light. I felt a great peace and feeling of trust about this. When I began to feel insecure that I had nothing to offer Him in return for His great love, He reminded Me of My own, which was a truly great love for Him now.

He led Me to a place of knowing that it was both of Us there, and not just Me alone who had these feelings. I trusted Him, and He trusted Me. Together, We went into more and more experience of One another. Enfolding Ourselves more and more in One another, We became more and more as One, yet Two, Our hearts entwined in a dance of wooing, growing One world between Us.

Orgasm after orgasm moved through Us with all of the delicious feelings of the individual orgasms they were. We savored them. Together, We grew in this expression of Our love. And in the expression of Our love, Heart began to flower more and more until He was ready to come forth. As Our Hearts overflowed with the passion of Our love, Heart conceived became Heart born in the world growing between Us.

Heart is Our love of the world growing between Us, made manifest in that world. Love is everywhere, and Heart helps Us to come together in that beautiful world. We are bound together now. Heart is Our child in Our garden, always held between Us in the safety of Our enduring love.

In time, Heart seeks another to keep Him company. Having grown enough to feel secure in His world, and having His own needs met, He welcomes another addition, which is His own mate springing forth from Our love.

When She comes, He knows Her already as the colors that were dancing in My eyes when I first met His Father. He is so happy to know that the newness of My first love has returned, this time to

Him, and is now going to be His mate forever.

And so Our world grows. Little by little, We are a growing family. Our garden is growing also, and what a delightful garden it is! Heart loves tending it for Us as home, and We love responding with sunshine, breezes, rains and warmth which brings forth even more beautiful abundance of growth and flowering. There is so much music and dancing for the love of it.

I held this dream so long and so strongly in My heart that I did not know how or why My heart could have acted like She did not know it, unless She did not trust Me when it did not seem to be coming into existence the way I had tried to nurture it to be.

Perhaps She thought I was too much a dictator when She actually got out there and saw that He had His own ways and ideas that didn't seem interested in hearing about this. Perhaps She wasn't as aligned with Me as I had hoped and thought. Perhaps She feared Him too much.

Perhaps She was more beautiful and alluring than either of Us realized and didn't know He would become so fastened onto Her there. Perhaps She did not know how to get Him to let go.

Perhaps She found Her own lack of self-assurance when He didn't respond the way Our desire wanted Him to. Perhaps She reflected My own lack of love for Myself and My own lack of faith in My dream. Perhaps, perhaps, perhaps... I only question Her gap.

I do have great love for Her and sympathy for Her situation, but something has been keeping Us apart that has never been resolved, and I ask Her to look at this with Me because that is My way. My way is love and not denial of things tossed outside into a gap, never to be looked at again. How did you get hooked up with the Father and agree to do this with Him?

I know You have always claimed to understand Him better than I did, love Him more than I did and be better for Him than I was. You felt Him there. You noticed He didn't like Me. If You felt Him so well, didn't You feel there was also something wrong in the feeling of Your liaison with Him? Why didn't You return to Me then and tell Me what You felt there?

You needed to return to Me and tell Me these things so that I could have understood then that He was not ready yet. You needed to tell Me these things so that I could have understood that He was like a small boy, still only interested in His own amusement, but that He had looked at You with interest.

The next step would have been relating, and You stayed until He did that with You instead of coming back and helping Me the way young girls help each other when they are first interested in a boy. Instead, You were like the friend who takes the boy for Herself and moves out of the friendship rather than face anything there.

You grew up with Him instead of letting Me grow up with Him and somehow didn't notice that this was not right, and that it would be Your turn next. To give Me no input for so long was not right, no matter what You want to say about it. You knew Me better than that. Why did You treat Me this way?

When You did return, finally, after so long, there was something wrong with the feeling in it. I was afraid that My daughter had been out there doing something that She should not have been doing, but You would not tell Me what it was, or anything about it. Apparently, You were afraid of My reaction, and with good reason, I suppose.

You shut Me out, and I did not know how to approach You or what to ask You after that. You seemed to slip away at every opportunity, and I am wondering if You were meeting Him in the darkness, secretly, even then. Were You having sex with Him already there and not telling Me? Did it just happen and You did not know how to tell Me, or was it calculated?

I wanted to trust You there and did not know I had any reason not to, but You stayed too long without explaining why You were there and what it was really about. Did I send You on a mission that was too big for You; one You couldn't accomplish? If so, You needed to come back to Me and let Me know that.

What did You think I was, an ogre who would not think of something else to do then; someone who insisted You had to succeed at this, or else? How could You know Me and love Me as I thought Our relationship was and not know this about Me?

Did He not let You go? Did He hold You prisoner there? If so, couldn't You have let Me know somehow? I had My feelings, but whenever I tried to get help from You in understanding them, You denied My interpretation there. Didn't You think I knew anything? Did You think You knew it all, or so much more than I did.

Did You think You knew it all so much better than Me that You could get out in front of Me and never look back? Were You even going to come home before You were thrown and fell there? If the mission was too big for You, why didn't You let Me know and take it as an indication that this might not be the right approach or that He might be too big for You and that it needed to be Me there first instead of You? We had never done this before. It wasn't written anywhere that it had to be this way. If it wasn't working, We could have gotten another plan.

By the time He finally came to Me, He already had an attitude of disinterest, as though there was someone else He could go to if it wasn't just right with Me. He was impatient and expected Me to know things already about Him that I did not know. He acted insulted and infuriated when I didn't know certain things in His presence.

He acted like He knew Me and I should know Him. Did You really stay by choice so long with such a boor or did You tell Him You were Me and give Him the impression He knew Me then, as well. Did You bring Him to Me only out of a guilt when He gave You the feeling that You were not enough there? Did You fool Him? Did You lead Him to Me, and in that guise, turn and face Him there, over the top of Me and hope He would never find out what else was there underneath You?

When He didn't like what He felt there, did You decide that it was Me He was feeling and didn't like there, jump away from Me, say You weren't a part of that and go hurriedly away with Him? Did You hope He would never look back and discover anything about what had happened there? Did You try and make sure He would never look back, or could never look back?

I think, daughter Heart, that You imprinted early not to be too much like Your Mother, or Your Father would not like You the way You wanted Him to, would not give You all of the attention and admiration You needed and wanted to grow into the life You wanted to have there and would not do all the things for You that You wanted Him to do. Don't You think there is something sickening in the feeling of seeing fathers too wrapped around the little finger of their daughters?

When He finally came, I was already withering, old feeling, hopeless, angry, frightened and bitter. I wish I knew if this was because I didn't get to grow up with Him and participate in the beginning sexual experiences with Him. I wonder what I would have been like if I had been able to grow up with Him, instead of you? It never looked right to Me when You came home, finally. You looked too old for Your age, too soon. I don't think it would have been that way if it had been Me there with Him, instead.

Male Heart has had problems with His sexuality, too. It looked to Him as if there was no mate left for Him but the old part of the Mother; the part that no one else wanted. From when He began looking in places other than You for a mate there is homosexual imprinting there, too, making this even more complicated for the fragmentation You have become now to find mates.

If You want to say that I shouldn't have let this happen to Me, or that I should have known better than to let this happen to Me as a way to not have sympathy for the situation, I will have to remind You that outlook can also be applied to You. Is that the only way You are suddenly going to say that I am parental as a way to not have to take responsibility for anything. What You are really saying there is that the parental part has to know better. You have a long path to take to help heal this, daughter Heart, and I hope You will move along it as much as You possibly can now.

A BASE LEVEL OF THE GAP

Sub-particles finally began to come in response to My long, aching pull for something to be there with My emptiness. Slowly, only a few at first, like random encounters, not often, but shocking and frightening when they did come because they slammed into Me. I experienced this, too, as part of My emptiness. Random encounters that meant nothing, said nothing, had no knowing of Me, or I of them, except pain.

I hated having encounters when I did not know they were coming or what it was going to be like. If it was not going to be pleasant, I didn't like it. I knew that. It imprinted early. And what I liked, I knew early too; something else, not this.

I had no control over My own slamming into something, and what slammed into Me did not either, apparently, but when they claimed to like it, I did not trust them anymore. They seemed to want to hurt Me, as though they resented Me for calling them present there. I did not like these encounters and thought it was hateful and unfair of them to find pleasure in My pain, as though punishing Me for drawing them into My miserable void.

I hated them. They were cold and harsh. I did not know what else there could be, but I began to have feelings in Myself of other ways; soft and warm, floating, taking more time; gentle encounters, not propelled and bombarding, not hurting.

Then things slowed down too much, without any movement perceptible there. This was equally insufferable; stultifying, compressing, suffocating and just as terrifying and enraging as the other extreme.

Could they not feel anything? I formed the impression that they could not. They are not like Me, I concluded. I hated them. I only wanted what I liked and did not want relationship the way it was happening to Me; gentle mist, drifting in the void, bombarded, slammed and blown by cold, harsh winds of unknown source, scattering My mist into nothingness again and again, as though it did not want Me there. I would have to struggle to recover, if I even could. I did not like it any more than it liked Me. It was hatred there.

It felt like I was being annihilated. I imprinted that existence was a struggle and that it was a struggle to hold onto anything I ever was, had or got. I imprinted that something could come from nowhere, without warning, and take it all away and annihilate Me without noticing or caring what happened there, or because it hated Me and wanted to. They imprinted that the environment was hostile because I hated them coming in on Me that way.

I struggled with feelings of wanting to go back out of existence, because I hated what was happening there. After loneliness, came relationship. Hatred was the first imprinted feeling I had about both, because it was not what I wanted.

There was heartbreak. The weight of it took Me down, and I did not know it. I held Myself frozen there so as not to feel the pain of My disappointment. After such an interminable time of longing for something to be there with Me, it had to be this; something I did not like, even hated with a coldness that made Me even more frozen and withdrawn.

I wanted to come forward, like a delicate flower, translucent as My mist, quivering at the nourishing drops of a dew falling upon its petals, but I could not. I did not even know I had petals to come forward. I never got that far before consciousness withdrew from Me, as though it did not like Me, either.

I was frozen and did not respond to it the way it wanted Me to. It was harsh and cold. It had frozen Me, I wanted to say to it there, but I had no voice with which to speak such things. I had no means to express Myself. It had to feel Me, or there was nothing to go on, and it did not. It hated Me, I was sure of that. Otherwise it wouldn't have been so harsh and cold toward Me.

I was imprinting in the photographic mists, lying in darkness to awaken later, when consciousness came to Me and touched Me with its light. The way that touch felt was all telling in terms of outcome.

I was like a magnetic mist, and consciousness was like radiation bombarding Me. It was unpleasant and seeming to want to blow Me out of existence. I felt blown away every time I had these encounters in the beginning. I had only glimmers of awareness when I had these encounters, but they were not pleasant glimmers. I did not know anything other than shocks of pain that I hated.

I tried to move along this path so as not to give hatred the upper hand as though it was the only thing happening there, but without moving the hatred, it never left Me any more than the terror did. I hated quickly when I did not like what was happening and was intolerant in many ways. I hated Myself for being intolerant and hated the intolerance toward Me.

I did not know it was possible that I had moved past others already by calling them there before they were ready. When I called them, I did not know there were others. I thought there was only Me, longing for what was not, which was companionship and relationship in My loneliness. I had no feeling I noticed there of anything except My desire to have something there with Me. I only noticed that what came did not seem to want existence or relationship.

I hated what first came in response to My longing. Later, when it said it felt pulled into a trap by Me, as though I never intended to let it go once I pulled it to Me, I could not understand the resentment these things I was encountering in the darkness had toward Me. My longing did not want anything there that did not want to be there with Me.

I could not understand why they wanted to hurt or kill Me instead of being there in pleasant relationship with Me. I could not understand why they would not want to come toward Me in a friendly manner instead of bombarding Me in that way. Why would they feel trapped by Me instead of pulled to Me and glad of it, as I had wanted it to be? I did not understand, and I did not have the means to get answers to any of My questions.

I had no means to relate to them when I encountered them bombarding Me in the darkness. I shut Myself to them as much as possible to avoid as much pain as possible. I could not get a hold of them. I resented their speed. I imprinted that they had to slow down to find the means to solve these problems. I hated it when they did slow down, because it was too much to the other extreme. They floated maddeningly near Me but did not come close. There was no attraction.

When I finally did find the means to get a hold of one, it was only through sexual attraction, and I did not like that. I imprinted that these particles, which were not really particles, were like angry, stinging bees who only alighted long enough to see what they could take.

We were no match, and I wanted them to leave as soon as

possible. Then I found Heart there with Me, but Heart did not love Me here, either. Heart was just an angry something, left behind by the particles that could not get free another way and broke loose however possible.

I felt stupid and naive and never wanted to let Myself be open that way again when I felt rejected for reasons I did not understand. I never really opened My heart again after that and did not know what was wrong when I was accused of being heartless.

I was always rejected and blamed. I imprinted that there was only coldness toward the dark, loneliness of My early experience, as though I was making a lot out of nothing, because nothing was all it was.

I could not move past this place without help. I was trapped in it, Myself. I hated needing help and was hated for needing help. He, as it had become to Me now, said that was My fault because I did not like His rage, and He moved away from Me even more then.

He never let Me know anything about Him that I wanted to know. He never let Me know anything about His origins or how it had felt to Him to come into existence. He just always was. I was letting Him know what it had been like for Me. He acted annoyed and disinterested. He hated hearing anything about it.

He gave Me the feeling that I should not be telling Him. It stirred rage in Him for calling Him when He did not want to be called. I gave in to Him for a long time because I was afraid of His rage. Even though it was not moving, I felt it there and felt its hatred. His hatred was turned against Me for not liking My experience in the darkness as a peaceful place without interference from others.

He said He was older than Me and knew better than Me. I did not see how He could be older than Me and not be ready for relationship, as I was. How much loneliness was it going to take before He would be ready to have someone else there? I did not think He could have been there, alone, as long as I was.

When He said He was there already, somewhere else, and didn't want Me there, I hated Him for this. I had no idea I was doing anything there that was right, and He never let Me know that I was. He only complained about Me interrupting His reverie of floating with My feelings and desire for relationship.

He never mentioned the part that had bombarded Me, but He said He was everything. I was apparently nothing, then, to Him, and that was just what I felt He was trying to make Me be. I hated Him for that, and He hated Me and would not admit it. I simmered and smouldered and smoked in dark hatred for Him there. He said it was My problem and went off to be chirpy and superficial somewhere else, somewhere where He could get away with it because He was believed by something that didn't have the wit to question.

He wanted Me to be independent so that I did not need relationship, only have it when He wanted to. This would then leave Him plenty of free time to drift in His reverie without being interrupted by Me needing Him. I did not want this. I wanted to find relationship that did things together, other than just have sex. This never worked. He always said I interrupted Him with My questions and observations that He did not want to hear. He did not like My emotions.

He had a different approach. His reverie was not supposed to have emotions stirring it up; only peace and calm. He avoided a lot this way, and I hated Him for that! He said I was consumed by questions and feelings and that I was not going to get the answers I needed unless I went along in My experience as I was having it now.

I could not let go, or forget, the way He wanted Me to to move along with Him there, and He hated Me for that. I had always My past with Me, no matter what experience I was having, and it became stronger than any other experience the longer it went on like this. No matter what experience We were having, I was always drowning inside of Myself and suffocating in the terror that I could not live. I needed to get free of this and hated Him for not helping Me with it. Sometimes it looked like He was going to help Me, but He only played with My terror in cruel ways.

Who cares what happened to you there! I did not know this was rage talking, because it hated the experience as much as I did and did not want to remember it, let alone ever go back to that place and re-experience anything about it. I thought it was right, light, even God talking there. It certainly was consciousness, and a consciousness that seemed more able to live than I ever was.

I tried to do what it said. I never succeeded, though. It made Me re-experience these horrors I lived with inside Myself over and over, as though shoving Me into it was somehow going to make Me understand it, or hate it as much as it did, and let go of it. It hated Me. As soon as I showed up, it was time to kill Me or get rid of Me any way possible. I was not wanted, and it let Me know that. It let Me know that so many times and in so many ways that I am not sure why I kept going there, except that I could not resist, as though I was suicidal, or something.

It was the light I thought it had. Over and over, like a moth to a flame, I went to My death at its hands. I did not know it was not God, either; only rage in His place. The gap was not something I knew I was in. It had happened, and I never knew there was another way of life.

I have dreamed of another way and wanted it for so long, but I never knew it was possible, as a reality, to have life the way I wanted it to be. I did not know how to get out of the place I was in. When others told Me there were other ways of living, I never experienced that. Whenever I got there, it always changed into My own kind of nightmare; if not immediately, soon enough that I had to live with the dread of it happening; forming in the mists around Me and precipitating into horrible, frightening realities I did not want to have.

The mist followed Me wherever I went. Others would say they were fine until I showed up, and then the mist drew 'round like a shroud and changed things as if in the night. I felt even more unwelcome then, as if there was no place I could go and no place I should go because of what was going to happen when I got there. What I wanted left Me and what I didn't want stayed until it killed Me. I got another start and repeated it again.

I was imprinted with hatred toward relationship and that it would be unpleasant from My very first encounters, before atoms had even formed yet. We were splitting apart more than We were forming bonds of relationship and being stuck together by forces We did not understand whether We wanted to be, or not. I was left with only the dream that it could be otherwise if the approach was right. If something looked like the right approach, it triggered a dream-like quality in Me of fantasies coming true. I was fooled over and over, they all degenerated rather quickly into the same thing, until now the only option for Me is to heal the gap that needs to be healed there.

This is the gap where rage and hatred were born. We could have been companions, but We went to war instead. Hatred is older than love, and only because it was not helped to become love did it remain as hatred on My side. What about your side?

This has been told over and over, and yet, how really major it was cannot be told in words very easily. Can you see how everything that has troubled the male-female relationship, and everything else, was there? Can you look back that far and feel that deep in order to move this? Do you want to?

I hesitate to tell My own point of view because it was not the same as others, but I need to move along with it, nonetheless. I moved past Heart and Body on more than one occasion. I hated Them for not moving along with Me in the ways I wanted to move there. To Me, They were know-nothings who had Their own agenda and wouldn't listen to anyone else. They were either aligned or opposed according to whether They agreed or disagreed on any given issue.

I thought it was not possible to get anything accomplished without alignment and did not like it that They were so vacillating in the name of freedom. I thought it was a lack of commitment to One another, and so Heart presence was not there strong enough to hold it together. It wasn't a matter of love to Me there, it was a matter of getting the job done, and the job at hand there was creating what We wanted to have in Our lives, since it appeared We now had lives.

They got angry over anything and left Me there with no movement toward Me for a long time, as though They did not need Me or even see any reason why I was there or needed to be there. I was hurt by this, but rage never moved about it. Instead, I gave Them nothing in return. They gave Me nothing, and We had long periods of nothing between Us.

I did not know We were coming together in the gap and making a Creation of war and strife, based on unquestioned impressions, without Our consciousness there to help, because Our denied rage was going after the Ones it wanted to give the rage to. Everyone was involved in this, not just My light.

The Mother also had Her own forces there, but they were less powerful than Ours and usually lost in battle. This is why We never minded going off into battle. We always thought We were going to win, even if We lost some people along the way. It didn't matter to Us. We didn't feel it that way because We had not grown to love One another in the first place.

We had given One another the gap only, in Our rage, and hated the results without knowing where they had come from. We hated war openly and gave people on Earth most of the blame for having wars.

God never came forward in any church sermons and said, " I caused these wars by not moving My rage."

It has been so long another version that many people cannot

believe it's God if I say it now, but those of you in the gap are hoping My light is involved so I can help you now, and you are not wrong.

I have moved this old rage already, but I have lost Will that needs to move along with Me on this. Because I have moved already, I know how it is going to heal. I have the visionary overview that Heart and Body originally did not like, because it made Them feel like They were being told what to do, but I want to move along with Them in another way now and have Them feel the rightness of this.

They have a lot of rage to move around being told what to do and not liking input from others who might know something They do not already know. I had a lot of rage to move around Them not listening to Me and then crying out in blame for Me when it was not the way They wanted it to be.

I hated that blame, because I had just as much toward Them. How dare They run past Me, consciousness, of all things, that gave Them the ability to know They even could run! I have raged and raged at Them for this, because They did not move along with Me. I had a plan, and They did not listen.

They moved past Me without conscious understanding of what They were doing or of what was causing Them to do it. I am having to come back now, so much later, and try to fix the mess They created originally. I have more rage to move in the lost Will that Spirit is the only One who knew and no One listened, not even the Mother, who could not seem to get ahold of Her emotions long enough to listen to reason.

I have moved past this position already, but I know there are others out there who have not and who need to move this rage to move along with Me because they are a part of My light also, albeit a long lost part. Most of them are dangerous in the small realms where they still have their power because they moved out of Me, holding the position I no longer hold there, believing no one listens to them and they are the only ones that know anything. They are not happy people, usually, and are not raging, either. They coldly hold it within themselves and make moves governed by this outlook.

They have to come back into Me, but it is not going to be easy to get them back after so long a time of being out there, holding a position that turned them even against Me, because they thought I was being too soft on the others when I did not come straightforward with how I felt there at the time. Feelings have not been moving in them, either, I notice, because they did not think they had to move feelings, only make reality the way they wanted it. I separated Myself from them, because I did not think I was loving there to have this opinion about everyone else.

I had denial spirits in Me already who had My denial in mind as well as everyone else's. Anytime they did not like My position, they moved past Me, too. They were more and more broken off from Me as I denied this viewpoint in Myself more and more and tried to move along only with the more "loving" parts of Myself that wanted to work it out with others and not be lacking in commitment.

I had feelings that were not moving of hating the backwardness of My other parts in not understanding My light. Why couldn't They handle holding back and not moving ahead so fast? Didn't They know They were going to last a long time and that Their moves needed to be the right moves to have the experience They wanted to have?

Holding emotions did not seem to be a problem for Me there, either. I just gave them some time, and they left Me. Where they went, I did not know. They were not with Me anymore, and that was all I noticed at the time.

Giving it more time was necessary in the beginning, but it needed to be filled in with things that were not happening there. There needed to be emotions moving and body sensations having the experience of getting accepted there. Acceptance, a little at a time, of My physicality would have helped Me to understand what was happening there. As it was, there was so much happening all at once that I couldn't make sense of it, and My light's position was to pull back and try to make sense of it, rather than have the experience and try to understand it that way.

This was because of My orientation. I did not understand what experience had to offer Me there. My light, in other words, did not know that physicality had things to teach Me, only that I had things to teach Him. He resented Me for this and did not let Me teach Him anything, because He was not moving His rage.

He feared Me, too, and did not let that show because He did not want to appear weaker than Me. He did not trust Me to value Him enough to give Him the place He wanted to have there. When He began posturing as though He wanted to overpower Me, I did not trust Him, either.

So quickly that He barely felt He had any, He moved past His fears into a rage that judged Me just as quickly. He had My light in Him already and was not giving it back, and so I could barely move faster than He could in these ways and not as fast as He could physically. He judged Himself to be faster than Me and viewed My slowness there as resistance to Him and resistance to joining Him in physicality.

He had no space for My light's need to go slower with physicality, and I suddenly did not look fast in consciousness to Him, either. He felt like a problem to My reverie, more than the Will even, and when He moved past Me, I was sure I no longer wanted Him near Me anyway. He had become too turbulent and was stirring Me in ways that lacked the quietude I had so been enjoying.

My light holding back and hovering outside of Body had an alignment with Him there that I was not admitting to. I did not like Him there, and so I did not enter into Him fully, but if I did not have some involvement, I would not have been hovering so nearby. I was watching what He had in mind very closely. I did not think it was loving, but I also had some outlook in Myself that was similar to His in that I had parts of Me that did not want to involve anyone else in what I was doing, either. I hated to think that it might not agree with Me and make limits that I didn't want to have there.

I did not notice My light pulling back there, but I did. I was frightened of His passion, ardor and sudden increase in intensity, and so was the female, in My opinion. It all seemed so sudden. We had had no time to get to know One another or ease into this thing at all.

He was a boor in My sight, and I did not like it that the Will appeared to be interested in Him. What felt so good to Her about Him was My light. She did not recognize it, and He was not crediting Me. He was stealing My place already and not being honest about how He got there. I hated Him for that and shoved it into lost Will immediately, because hatred was not love or the feeling I wanted to have in My reverie.

He wanted to move so quickly into sex, and I was not sure how this felt to Me, to get so suddenly, physically intense after so long a time of only finding pleasure in freely drifting with no focus or sudden, intense passion such as this. I wanted to go more slowly and ease into it a little at a time. He felt driven up immediately and not willing to hold back for anyone, especially not Me.

He was raging with a frustration of held back sexual energy, and at the same time He was screaming about held back sexual energy, He was moving toward having more and more sex all the time. I did not realize this immediately, but I came to understand that since He had literally moved past My light without gaining an alignment with Me, He could never be satisfied.

I delighted in this for a long time as His punishment for moving past Me and as what He deserved for His behavior. This manifested as many diseases, too, and I did not help heal them. If any of His partners, and there were soon many, got the diseases, well, they deserved it for going along with Him and allowing Him to tear them apart in His rages instead of staying with Me.

I had blame for Him for a long time. It did not seem possible that I could have withheld My light. It looked to Me like He had shortchanged Me while I had not reciprocated. I had not short-changed Him, so I was more loving than He was, or so I thought for a long time, but I had not given Him My loving light. I had given Him denied light full of judgment, sexual curiosity and prurient interest in this.

I had given Him My fear, too, that He was wrong and My light did not accept Him or approve of Him there. I did not notice My light raging at Him in the gap as other than justified for what He had done to Me. I did not know the origin of My rage. For a long time, He just looked like a pervert to Me who had repeatedly pushed past My light and given the Will more painful reproductive experiences than She needed, given Her delicate state.

When the Will appeared to like it, I hated the Will for giving Her sexual interests priority over Her delicate condition, Her pain and all of the other things She complained to Me about when We had private moments together, which were not often compared to how often Body dragged Her into the scenes He wanted to have. Had She only pretended to My light that She did not like what was happening to Her?

It looked perverse and more and more twisted to Me. What I thought would take form like delicate, colorful flowers was now bestial, hairy and dripping with things I did not like the looks or smell of compared to what I thought was going to happen there. I was grossed out by what was happening there and did not like the reflection that I had given sex a bad name by pulling back, disapproving and saying it was wrong. I had no idea it was going to be like that.

I split with Him there by holding My position that I was only being cautious, taking My time and trying to understand first. He did not like My light's position there but did not give His own position. He only condemned Mine. This did not help Me understand what He felt was wrong with Me and My approach. I was just moving a little slower than He was, that was all, until His urgency suddenly pushed past Me and I found Myself floating out from Body into space.

When I noticed that even the ones who had tried to stay with Me could not hold themselves back sexually, either, and gave in to Him from time to time, I thought they were all a sinful lot, and I had many raging fantasies about what was going to happen to them then. They were often mutilated and burned as witches until most of them now innately feel that they had better not open up to sexual feelings or there is going to be a problem coming from somewhere. This is something that needs rage movement first and then other feelings need noticing there.

He gave Me no place of My own from which I could come from My own point of view. He gave Me the impression that My light did not understand His physical drives, was holding Him back and had labeled Him wrong and judged Him already. A huge split, or gap, developed between Us. Before We had time to understand more, it had gone past the place of feeling healable. My rage was immense, and later, so was My fear of impotence when He did not embody Me in those places.

He decided to attack Me and give Me no place. If there was only going to be one place, then He was going to be the One to fill it. He hesitated to attack Me openly, though, so it went into the gap. The gap between Our open presentation and the rest of Our agenda was getting larger and larger and becoming filled with more and more pieces of Ourselves that We did not want to come to light. How far into the gap it went depended upon how much hatred and how little love was there.

When He attacked Me, I began to defend Myself by hiding behind His body presence in places, trying to pull strings and manipulate His consciousness to lean in certain ways that were not against Me. I usually did this by pointing out other participants and saying it was Their fault, really. We hated these places in Ourselves and did not move love into them for a long time.

Not very mature sounding, I know, but I was not very mature then. I have learned a lot, and My feeling now is that I want to move along to help others with what I know. Whether others can receive Me or not depends on movement of the old charge about being told anything by Me that they do not already know.

There are many out there who claim to be channeling Me, but they have had nothing new to say for so long that I must not be evolving, which I know is not true. They have old imprinting that says I had to know everything already or I wasn't fit to be God. It's absurd if you think about it, but consciousness has not been able to say much about how the mind pretends to think. Openness in the body to receive Me has not been much since Body split off and went past Me so long ago.

He hated Me for many reasons, but holding Him back was the main one. He felt holding Him back any longer was not right since He had been there for so long already, unable to move. He forgot that He was there as My light. He had form, yes, in that My light had form as light, but as He developed more Body consciousness that could move, He began to see Himself as something separate from what He had started out as.

As Body that could move the way He wanted to move then, He was not there that long before He went past Me with an angry judgment that I was holding back, trying to hold Him back and was not going to accept His presence as an equal to My own. I wasn't, either, because I did not like His separatist ideas and the way He was treating Me there, as if there was suddenly no integration between Us anymore.

He began to fear that I had separatist ideas of My own, separating Myself from what I didn't like about Him and making Myself appear to be better than Him. He imprinted this in response to My slowness in accepting His new awareness but did not notice how much of Me was with Him already. He took that for granted and interpreted that as His own light now.

His rage did not move. His rage moved past Me, out ahead, and this split between Body and Spirit is all that is known on Earth. He left His grief and terror behind in so doing and His Heart, too. He felt there was no place for Him that He wanted to have and His rage was going to make a place and get there first, before I took it from Him.

I found Him insufferable in this position and so did not move to help Him have it. Thus, I was seen as holding back and not moving to empower Him with My light. This was not right on My part, because it gave Him the opportunity to imprint without My input there, but I was busy with My own unmoved rage telling Me I did not care what He did out there, as long as I protected My space and kept Him out of it.

I blamed emotions then as the reason We did not move past Our positions there. I felt that emotions were self-centered and couldn't see, or didn't care about, the bigger picture they were messing up. I hated the Mother for everything that was not right then, because it all looked like it was not right because of emotions that had gotten in the way. I did not blame Her in the form of the

Mother yet, though. I didn't even know We had a presence in that form yet. But by the time I met Her, I was already imprinted against Her.

She had no chance with Me from the beginning, because I had no openness to receive Her any more than the rest. No one was going to tell Me anything in My unmoving rage. This rage was held back more than anything else because I had the least acceptance for it. Next, terror was held back because rage terrified Me and then heartbreak, or grief, because it felt nothing was working out the way I wanted it to, and I couldn't stand looking at that.

Because I thought rage was first, rage had accorded itself the parental position without My even knowing it. This was further bolstered by the imprint that it was the only one that knew anything and no one else did. It hated Me for not letting it have free rein and hated My other emotions for not getting out of its way and letting it happen the way it was meant to. This is rage's imprinting, and it has not moved much since it broke loose and got out there without Me.

It has to move now in more ways than one, and off of Earth is not wrong in terms of the form it has had for so long. It cannot move off Earth in terms of all the essence held there, because that would not be right place. So, getting this rage moving is going to mean a lot of essence coming in that you are going to need to balance in yourselves. Not moving past it is a major exercise in getting it moving. Rage has not liked emotional movement, because it has imprinting that this is not the right approach to take. Only the rage that is not going to move now needs to move to another planet to work this out because it needs more time.

Trapped by its own imprinting that says it is the only one who knows anything, it has to be its own idea that it should move. Being pointed out by others does not make it feel like cooperating there. It has to go away and move in private so that it does not even have to admit that it is moving at first. It has fear underneath that it might have to get off of its old position if it moves very much of this rage, which runs it into a circle, back to its old imprinting that says it can't be wrong and so on.

Many times, this rage has preferred to discredit the input rather than risk feeling it might be exposed as wrong. It has had little conscious mind there to help it understand that it is not a matter of right and wrong anymore. It has been so defensive that it has been sifting all input according to whether it thinks it is going to come out looking right or wrong in the end instead of looking at the input.

I had nowhere to go with My rage except outside of My love at the time, and rage has never felt included in My light because of that. I had a feeling at the time that love did not include rage. I did not think it included terror or grief, either, really, but I let it in more than I did rage. My light is not empowering rage in a state of denial by denying it anymore. It has to come in. It is only a matter of time.

It is right time to move into the nuances of emotion and find out what has been overlooked there. Whatever Our imprinting has been, We took it in and know what it is, and so, who else can take responsibility for it but Us. It is not a question anymore of who was victimized more than the next person. All of that needs to move as it needs to move.

The next step is to notice that interpretation played a large role in making assumptions and judgments. These interpretations, assumptions and judgments have been reality, and for the most part, no one questioned this.

The problems that arose from this arose mostly from not realizing that what We were going on was not all there was to the situation and was mostly just what We interpreted the situation to be according to what We knew of Ourselves, which was not much.

We viewed One another as limiting to Our own ideas of how We wanted it to be. So early We hated limits that it made Me think it was not new there and that We had hated the void as limiting Us to nothingness, and that instead of moving Our fear around Our own feeling of powerlessness and insignificance there, We gained Our existence by moving past that fear into a rage that wrested past all of those feelings of being limited and held back, of not knowing and of fearing what the darkness might hold, into forward thrusting movement and light, intolerant of any limits.

Going on what We had to go on was not the wrong approach as long as We moved along to find out what else there was. In most cases this did not happen, however, because of the distrust that arose immediately upon contacting something We did not like. Distrust, as a form of fear, grew into hatred and even rage and terror the longer it went on without getting any help understanding itself.

This has not moved. There has been too much terror here that if We cannot or do not know what reality really is, We cannot know what to do or how to handle Ourselves. This terror has to be faced to notice how much of an opening this left for the "voice of authority" to step in and say that it did know. Conformity has been another way to avoid terror because, "We cannot be wrong if We're all doing it."

It is necessary to notice more than what has been noticed. It is necessary to notice that under the reactionary anger and blame toward others and all the charges in it that say it is because of them that We are not alright the way We are and not enough, and that it is because of the voice that is oppressing Us that We cannot do better, there is a fear in Us that all of this might be true and that instead of being able to battle it out there, We're going to have to face it within.

It is not possible to move past living the repetition of your imprinting without making changes in the actual imprinting itself. No matter how hard you try, it only repeats. This is because nothing has had more power than the subconscious on Earth. It has had the most presence in the essence and the most mass in the brain. This imprinting does not lead to survival in the end, only temporarily, even if it has appeared to be a very long temporarily.

Once your Original Cause imprints, and how they were put into place, are known to you, you do not have to move along those paths anymore unless you want to, but it is necessary to move the emotion that has held this in place as the way it is, the way it has to be and always will be. This imprinting has been very resistant and defensive in the past. I hope it will not be this time.

The healing of the gap is what I see in My vision of love, and I hope that you want to see yourself there with Me. Until Indigo reveals itself,

Selah

IMPRINTING

A Healing of the Chakras

is the seventh in a series of books
channelled by Ceanne DeRohan

The other books are:

RIGHT USE OF WILL
Healing and Evolving the Emotional Body

ORIGINAL CAUSE 1
The Unseen Role of Denial

ORIGINAL CAUSE 2
The Reflection Lost Will Has to Give

EARTH SPELL
The Loss of Consciousness on Earth

HEART SONG
Vibrating Heartlessness to Let Heart in

LAND OF PAN
The Loss of Power and Magic on Earth

These books need to be read in order. Getting ready for the sequels involves moving along with the material in *Right Use of Will* enough to know if this information is right for you.

These books let you know your *Original Cause* by helping you access belief systems lost in the subconscious long ago, yet influencing your life every day.

We appreciate it that you have bought this book. If you are interested in others and cannot get them through your local store, you may write us, Four Winds Publications, at the address in the front of the book for information on how to order. Please enclose a Self Addressed Stamped Envelope. Thank you.

$15.00 FOUR WINDS PUBLICATIONS